VEGETARIAN
Soups for All Seasons

Also by Nava Atlas

Vegetarian Express
(coauthored with Lillian Kayte)

Vegetariana

Vegetarian Celebrations

American Harvest

VEGETARIAN
Soups for All Seasons

A TREASURY OF BOUNTIFUL LOW-FAT SOUPS AND STEWS

Revised Edition

Written and illustrated by

NAVA ATLAS

Little, Brown and Company

Boston   New York   London

Revised Edition

Atlas, Nava.
    Vegetarian soups for all seasons : a treasury of bountiful low-fat soups and stews /
        Nava Atlas.— Rev. ed.
        p. cm.
    Includes index.
    ISBN 0-316-05733-9
    1. Soups. 2. Stews. 3. Vegetarian cookery. 4. Cookery,
International.   I. Title.
    TX757.A85 1996
    641.8'13—dc20   95-49915

10 9 8

Printed in the United States of America

CONTENTS

ACKNOWLEDGMENTS

Thanks to the following contributors for their tasty soup recipes: Toni Atlas for Moroccan-Style Vegetable Stew; Commander's Palace Restaurant in New Orleans for Creole Eggplant Soup; Gary Raheb, in memory of his mother, Grace Raheb, for Cream of Lettuce Soup; and Neil Trager for Hot-and-Sour Oriental Vegetable Soup.

This book began its life as a diminutive self-published volume. I'd like to thank those who helped launch the project: my husband, Harry Chaim Tabak, who gave me the confidence to go ahead and do it; Bob Holzapfel; and Gil Plantinga.

And now, having completed this freshly redesigned and expanded edition, I'd like to acknowledge Joe Tantillo, for his typographic excellence; and all those supportive people I have enjoyed working with at Little, Brown and Company over the years, including Abigail Wilentz, Donna Peterson, Steve Snider, Martha Kennedy, and, saving the best for last, my editor, Jennifer Josephy.

VEGETARIAN
Soups for All Seasons

INTRODUCTION

Soups have always held a very prominent spot in my culinary repertoire. I regard them as just about the most rewarding yet easiest things a cook can prepare. Here the cook has a wonderfully diverse range of possibilities and results: A soup might be familiar and soothing, evoking memories of the warmth and comfort of a childhood home, or it might be a mélange of sophisticated flavors that meld together in a pleasantly unexpected way. Or, with a bit less liquid and a tad more chunkiness of texture, the result is stew — a savory and satisfying one-pot meal.

Best of all, soups are welcome at any time of year, reflecting the harvest of each season. A soup can transform the lush variety of summer's fruits and vegetables into a most refreshing elixir; few dishes can better brighten a humdrum winter day than a bowl of hot soup; and finally, soup can be a splendid showcase for the tender new produce of spring or the bounty of fall's harvest.

From one soup-lover to another, here are one hundred soups for you to choose from. The soups presented here are in keeping with today's emphasis on low-fat, high-fiber foods. It almost goes without saying that you need not be a vegetarian to enjoy these recipes — with inspiration coming from around the globe, they are for everyone who appreciates fresh and flavorful seasonal produce, whole grains, healthful beans (as well as lentils and peas), and the judicious use of herbs, spices, and other seasonings. Not to mention the wonderful aromas that a big pot of simmering soup imparts, whetting the appetite like nothing else can.

COOKING NOTES

EQUIPMENT

The soups in this book are simple enough to require only the most basic of kitchen equipment. Aside from a large soup pot or Dutch oven, of course, the items needed are standard to most any kitchen: wooden spoons for stirring, a colander for washing leeks and leafy vegetables, a grater, measuring utensils, and good knives. For the devoted soup cook, I heartily recommend a food processor for pureed soups; the food processor is also useful for making occasional grating easier and quicker.

FREEZING

Some soups freeze well, but others lose much of their flavor and texture. Thick winter bean and grain soups do well, as do broths and stocks. Freezing often changes the texture of a smooth puree, making it more watery. Avoid freezing soups that contain potatoes or lentils, both of which turn quite mushy. I don't recommend freezing soups containing raw ingredients, as in certain chilled soups. The soups in this book generally don't yield such enormous quantities as to warrant long-term storage of leftovers. I prefer finishing most soups while they are fresh rather than after they have been frozen and thawed.

SOUP TEXTURES AND CONSISTENCIES

Here is an area that is rarely discussed in the presentation of soup recipes and yet is almost as important to tailor to the individual recipe as is seasoning. Soup making, though essentially very easy, is an inexact science. For instance, what one cook considers a large potato might be a medium one to another, and so the amount of water or liquid called for in a recipe might not always yield precise results. The soup recipes here often remind the cook to adjust the consistency or thickness, and this, like salting, should be done according to the cook's preference. Some soups are meant to be very thick, and others to be thin and brothy, but most seem to fall somewhere in between, and thus may be tailored to your liking.

A WORD ABOUT BEANS

I consider beans of all types an intrinsic part of vegetarian soup making. They are not only a superb low-fat, high-fiber protein source, but they also add a great deal of flavor and texture to soups. In instances where beans are the primary ingredient of a soup, such as in Black Bean Soup or Spicy Chili Bean Soup, dry beans are used, so that they become the base of the soup.

In most other cases, however, I give the option for using cooked or canned beans if the beans are to be added later in the cooking process.

In many cases where one cup or two of cooked beans are needed, I specify canned beans. It is not worth the time and trouble to cook this small amount, unless, of course, you cook extra for later use or for freezing. In the case of chickpeas, I almost always recommend the use of the canned variety. Somehow, their taste and texture are better than when they are home-cooked. They also take an inordinately long time to cook — two to three hours. When using canned beans, I recommend draining and rinsing them of their salty liquid.

SEASONINGS FOR SOUPS

The right balance of seasoning, to lend depth of flavor, is particularly crucial for vegetarian soups, where even the use of a good vegetable stock may not be enough to create a complete, full-bodied flavor. The success of a vegetarian soup depends on using a variety of flavorings, adding dried seasonings early in the cooking process (and, conversely, adding fresh herbs at the end), and tasting often to adjust seasonings.

Quantities of seasonings given in soup recipes — in this book or others — should be tailored to individual tastes. As a perennial soup enthusiast, I have always loved to experiment with a pinch of this spice, a quarter teaspoon of this herb, and a half teaspoon of that. That's part of the fun and artistry of making soup. After motherhood intervened, I enjoyed the practicality of making a big pot of soup that would last several days, but I began leaning toward recipes that could be made simply and quickly. The best time-saver I discovered was eliminating the need for measuring minute quantities of many herbs and spices and instead using purchased seasoning mixes.

There are many blends and brands around, and they are wonderfully suited to use in soups, where small quantities of many seasonings add up to the zesty flavor needed to make any soup taste great. Feel free to experiment with the many varieties available. Here are the seasoning mixes I use most often in making soups:

Curry powder (good quality) or garam masala: Purchase this blend from a spice shop, natural food store, or Indian grocery, if possible; at least avoid supermarket store brands, which are too flat and bland, and choose the Spice Islands brand. Use your sense of smell — curry powder should be fragrant and pungent.

Italian herb mix: A blend of several herbs such as oregano, thyme, marjoram, and rosemary — this is commonly available at specialty outlets as well as supermarkets.

Salt-free herb-and-spice seasoning mix: The savory blend of many different herbs and spices eliminates the need for excessive salting. This is an all-purpose way to add a complex flavor to soups. There are several good brands available in supermarkets and natural food stores. My favorite from the supermarket is salt-free Mrs. Dash Table Blend; from the natural food store, the aptly named Spike is a great product. There are other good brands; experiment with them and make good use of whichever you prefer.

Lemon-pepper: This mix gives a pleasant, lemony bite to Oriental soups and vegetable purees. Available in several brands in supermarkets and specialty outlets.

Here are some other seasoning tips:

• Add salt toward the end of the cooking to give the other flavors a chance to develop and thus avoid oversalting. Salt a little at a time, stir in thoroughly, and taste frequently.

• Those who need to limit their intake of salt might try adding lemon juice for added zest.

• Where appropriate, a small amount of dry wine adds nice depth of flavor. I use wine in some of the soups, but you might like to experiment with it in other recipes.

• Most important, use the amount of seasoning given here as a guide. Use more or less as suits your taste.

EXPLANATION OF NUTRITIONAL ANALYSIS

All breakdowns are based on one serving. When a recipe gives a range in the number of servings, e.g., 6 to 8 servings, the analysis is based on the average number of servings, in the case of this example, 7 servings.

When more than one ingredient is listed as an option (i.e., grated reduced-fat cheddar cheese or cheddar-style soy cheese), the first ingredient is used in the analysis. Usually, the option ingredient will not change the analysis significantly.

Ingredients listed as optional (such as "reduced-fat sour cream or low-fat yogurt for topping, optional") are not included in the analyis.

When salt is listed "to taste," its sodium content is not included in the analysis.

STOCKS AND BROTHS

The absence of a strong-flavored meat stock makes the preparation of tasty meatless soups a challenge, but honestly not a very difficult one. Many ethnic cuisines produce classic soups that in their intrinsic form are completely vegetarian. True, almost any soup can benefit from a good stock to really round out its flavor, but I place fresh and flavorful ingredients and creative seasoning above stock in contributing to the success of a soup. I would venture to say that most of the soup recipes in this book will work as well using water (with perhaps the occasional boost from a vegetable bouillon cube or two) as they will with a stock; still, it's useful to have stocks on hand when they're needed and to have a few basic recipes to refer to.

Following are a handful of stocks and broths, the first two of which are suitable as soup bases. The remaining ones, in the Oriental tradition, make good broths to be eaten on their own or lightly embellished.

Light Vegetable Stock

Makes about 6 cups

This is a basic stock that may be used in place of water in most any vegetable soup to give added depth of flavor. It's also a good way to use up vegetables that are limp or less than perfectly fresh.

7 cups water
1 large onion, chopped
1 large carrot, sliced
2 large celery stalks, sliced
1 medium potato, scrubbed and diced
1 cup coarsely shredded white cabbage
Salt to taste
2 teaspoons Italian herb mix

Place all the ingredients in a large soup pot. Bring to a simmer, then simmer gently, covered, over low heat for 40 to 45 minutes, or until the vegetables are quite tender. Strain the stock through 3 layers of cheesecloth.

Calories: 37	Total fat: 0 g	Protein: 1 g
Carbohydrate: 8 g	Cholesterol: 0 g	Sodium: 21 mg

Onion or Leek and Garlic Broth

Makes about 6 cups

This broth may be used as an extra-flavorful soup stock or as an alternative, with a little extra kick, to Light Vegetable Stock (page 7). It's also a soothing remedy for the common cold!

1 tablespoon canola oil

1 large onion, chopped, or 2 medium leeks, white parts only, cut into ¼-inch rings

4 to 6 cloves garlic, minced

6 cups water

¼ cup dry red wine

Salt to taste

⅛ teaspoon freshly ground pepper, optional

Heat the oil in a large heavy saucepan. If using leeks, separate the rings and rinse them well to remove grit. Add the onion or leeks and sauté over moderate heat until golden. Add the garlic and continue to sauté until the onion or leeks brown lightly. Add the water, wine, salt, and optional pepper, and bring to a boil. Cover and simmer over low heat for 30 to 40 minutes. You may leave the onions and garlic in if you wish, or strain the stock through a fine sieve or cheesecloth.

Calories: 42	Total fat: 2 g	Protein: 0 g
Carbohydrate: 3 g	Cholesterol: 0 g	Sodium: 25 mg

Onion: Humble kindred of the lily clan, rooted from oblivion by Alexander the Great and bestrewn by him, along with learning, to the civilised world, thus lending a touch of wisdom and sophistication to the whole.

— Della Lutes
The Country Kitchen, 1938

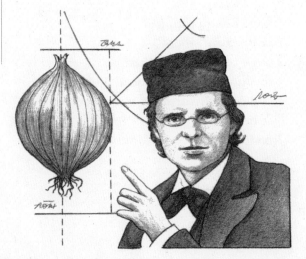

Simple Miso Broth

Makes about 6 cups

Miso is a nutritious, high-protein product fermented from soybeans and salt (or a combination of soybeans, grains, and salt). Available at all natural food stores and Oriental groceries (as is the sea vegetable kombu), pungent-tasting miso is most commonly used to make simple broths. Here is a basic recipe, which really should be considered a soup in itself rather than as a stock for making other soups. Note that once the miso is stirred into water, it should not be boiled, otherwise its beneficial enzymes will be destroyed.

6 cups water
2 strips of kombu (sea vegetable),
    each 3 by 5 inches
2 to 4 tablespoons miso, to taste

Combine the water and kombu in a soup pot and bring to a simmer. Remove the kombu. Dissolve the desired amount of miso in just enough warm water to make it pourable. Stir into the broth and remove from the heat. Serve at once.

Variations: Embellish miso broth with any of the following:

• Diced tofu

• Cooked Oriental noodles

• Finely chopped scallions

• Grated fresh daikon radish or white turnip

• Crisp cucumber, seeded and grated

Calories: 18	Total fat: 0 g	Protein: 1 g
Carbohydrate: 2 g	Cholesterol: 0 g	Sodium: 0 mg

Basic Dashi
(Japanese Kombu and Shiitake Mushroom Broth)

Makes about 6 cups

Along with miso broth, dashi is another traditional Japanese stock that may be embellished in a number of ways, or eaten very simply. It also makes a good base for certain Oriental vegetable soups. Look for the sea vegetable kombu and dried shiitake mushrooms in Oriental groceries or in natural food stores.

6 cups water
2 strips of kombu (sea vegetable),
    each about 3 by 7 inches
6 to 8 dried shiitake mushrooms

Combine the water and kombu in a soup pot. Bring to a simmer, then remove the kombu. Add the mushrooms to the stock and remove from the heat. Let stand for 30 minutes. Remove the mushrooms from the stock with a slotted spoon. Trim them of their tough stems and save them for another use or slice them and use them in the broth.

Variations:

DASHI WITH NOODLES: Simply cook a quantity of Oriental noodles in the stock. Once they are al dente, remove the soup from the heat, season to taste with natural soy sauce, and serve immediately. Garnish each serving with some finely chopped scallion.

DASHI WITH MISO AND VEGETABLES: Use the broth to simmer any quantity of thinly sliced vegetables such as carrot, cabbage, daikon radish, or turnip. Once the vegetables are just done, add 2 to 4 tablespoons of miso, to taste, dissolved in just enough warm water to make it pourable. Stir in the sliced shiitake mushrooms from the preparation of the stock. Remove from the heat and serve at once.

Calories: 15	Total fat: 0 g	Protein: 0 g
Carbohydrate: 3 g	Cholesterol: 0 g	Sodium: 61 mg

Oriental Mushroom Broth

Makes about 6 cups

This strong broth is a great flavor-booster for Chinese-style vegetable soups but is also a very pleasing broth to be eaten on its own. Vary it by using any of the embellishments suggested under Simple Miso Broth (page 9).

2 teaspoons sesame oil
1 small onion, minced
1 clove garlic, minced
6 cups water
8 to 10 dried shiitake mushrooms
1 to 2 tablespoons soy sauce or tamari, or
    to taste

Heat the oil in a large heavy saucepan. Add the onion and garlic and sauté over medium heat until the onion is golden. Add the water, mushrooms, and soy sauce or tamari. Bring to a simmer, then simmer gently, covered, for 15 minutes. Remove from the heat and let stand another 15 minutes. Strain through a fine sieve. Reserve the mushrooms, trimming them first of their tough stems. Save them for another use or slice them and return them to the broth.

Calories: 34	Total fat: 2 g	Protein: 1 g
Carbohydrate: 4 g	Cholesterol: 0 g	Sodium: 253 mg

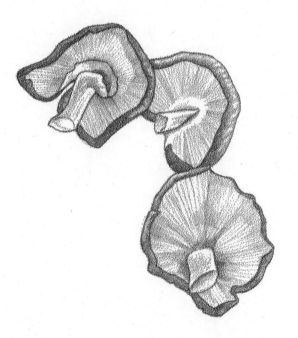

F · A · L · L

Autumn is an inviting time to make soup. In early to mid-season, the rich colors and lively flavors of the harvest can be shown off to great advantage in a warming tureen of soup. Later in the season, a tasty bowl of soup is a heartwarming way to temper the effects of chilly weather.

Baked Onion Soup

6 servings

Ceramic crocks with handles are the ideal bowls for this soup, but any type of ovenproof bowl will do. Miso makes a robust base for this classic soup, in place of the customary meat stock. For more on miso, see page 9, under Simple Miso Broth.

2 tablespoons canola oil
8 medium onions, quartered and thinly
    sliced
2 cloves garlic, minced
5 cups water
¼ cup dry red wine
1 teaspoon dry mustard
2 to 4 tablespoons miso, to taste,
    dissolved in ⅓ cup water (see note)
French bread, as needed
1½ cups grated reduced-fat mozzarella
    cheese or mozzarella-style soy cheese

Heat the oil in a soup pot. Add the onions and sauté over medium-low heat until they are golden. Add the garlic and continue to sauté slowly until the onions are lightly and evenly browned. Add the water, wine, and mustard. Bring to a simmer, then simmer gently, covered, for 15 minutes. Stir in the dissolved miso and remove from the heat. Allow the soup to stand for another 15 minutes.

Preheat the oven to 350 degrees.

Slice the bread into 1-inch-thick slices, allowing 1 slice per serving. Bake for 15 minutes, or until dry and crisp.

To assemble the soup, place a slice of bread in each ovenproof bowl and ladle a serving of soup over it. Sprinkle about ¼ cup of the grated cheese over each. Place the bowls on 1 or 2 cookie sheets so that they will be easier to handle. Bake the soup for approximately 10 minutes, or until the cheese is thoroughly melted. Serve at once.

Note: If you're unfamiliar with the intense flavor of miso, you might want to start with only 2 tablespoons, dissolved in half the water recommended above. Taste the soup, then add more dissolved miso to your taste if you'd like a stronger flavor.

Calories: 293	Total fat: 11 g	Protein: 13 g
Carbohydrate: 32 g	Cholesterol: 16 g	Sodium: 260 mg

Cream of White Vegetables

8 servings

A super-smooth, pale puree with a colorful garnish, this soup epitomizes both comfort and elegance. If you can, use the big pure white onions that are abundant in the fall.

2 tablespoons canola oil
1½ pounds white onions (if unavailable, substitute yellow onions), chopped
3 large potatoes, peeled and diced
2 to 3 cloves garlic, minced
1½ pounds white turnip, peeled and diced, divided
Salt and white pepper to taste
¼ to ½ cup low-fat milk or soy milk

Garnish:
1 teaspoon canola oil
2 tablespoons water
1 large red bell pepper, finely diced
½ cup frozen green peas, thawed
3 scallions, sliced
¼ cup chopped fresh parsley

Heat the oil in a soup pot. Add the onions and sauté over medium heat, covered, stirring occasionally, about 15 minutes, or until limp. Add the potatoes, garlic, and turnip, reserving and setting aside 1 cup of the turnip dice. Add enough water so that the vegetables are not quite covered. Bring to a simmer, then simmer gently until the vegetables are tender, about 35 to 40 minutes.

Transfer the vegetables to a food processor or blender with a slotted spoon and puree in batches until very smooth. Transfer back to the soup pot; stir in enough milk or soy milk to achieve a thick but fluid consistency. Reheat very gently while preparing garnish.

For the garnish, heat the oil and water slowly in a medium-sized skillet. Add the bell pepper dice along with the reserved turnip dice. Cover and "sweat" over medium heat until crisp-tender, about 7 minutes. Add the peas, scallions, and parsley, and steam, covered, about 5 minutes more, adding a bit more water if the skillet gets dry.

Ladle the soup into bowls and divide the garnish among them, placing some in the center of each bowl of soup.

| Calories: 139 | Total fat: 3 g | Protein: 3 g |
| Carbohydrate: 23 g | Cholesterol: 0 g | Sodium: 53 mg |

New England Clam-less Chowder

4/28 11-20 Nah -   6 to 8 servings

Tofu, sautéed to a chewy, crisp texture, stands in for clams in this classic American soup.

1 tablespoon canola oil
2 teaspoons soy sauce or tamari
4 ounces firm tofu, finely diced
1 tablespoon soy margarine
1 large onion, finely chopped
2 celery stalks, finely diced
2 tablespoons unbleached white flour
4 cups Light Vegetable Stock (page 7) or
   water *Chicken Broth*
3 medium potatoes, scrubbed and diced
3 cups fresh corn kernels, scraped off cob
   (from about 3 large ears)
½ ¼ teaspoon dried thyme
½ ¼ teaspoon dried summer savory or
   marjoram
1 2 cups low-fat milk or soy milk, or as
   needed
Salt and freshly ground pepper to taste

Heat the oil and soy sauce or tamari slowly in a medium-sized skillet. Stir the diced tofu in quickly to coat, then turn the heat up to medium high. Sauté, stirring frequently, until browned and crisp on all sides, about 12 to 15 minutes. When done, remove from the heat and set aside until needed.

In the meantime, heat the margarine in a soup pot. Add the onion and celery and sauté over moderate heat, stirring occasionally, until the onion is golden, about 10 minutes. Sprinkle in the flour a little at a time. Slowly stir in the stock or water, then add the potato dice, corn kernels, and dried herbs. Bring to a simmer, then simmer gently, covered, until the potatoes are tender and the corn kernels are done, about 20 to 25 minutes.

With the back of a wooden spoon, mash a small amount of potatoes to thicken the base. Then add milk or soy milk as needed; the soup should be semithick but not overly dense. *Tofu in.* Slowly bring to a gentle simmer, then season to taste with salt and pepper. If time allows, let the soup stand off the heat for an hour or two before serving, then heat through as needed.

Calories: 200	Total fat: 5 g	Protein: 7
Carbohydrate: 32 g	Cholesterol: 3 g	Sodium: 184 mg

Yukon Gold Potato Soup with Roasted Garlic and Red Peppers

☆ 11-20

6 to 8 servings

Though this soup is very low in fat, the buttery flavor of Yukon Gold potatoes makes it taste rich and luscious. Roasted garlic and red peppers add a deep, smoky flavor.

Make ½.

1 large or 2 medium whole heads garlic
1 tablespoon canola oil
1 cup finely chopped onion
6 to 7 medium Yukon Gold potatoes, peeled and diced
1 cup peeled, diced apple (use a soft cooking apple such as Cortland)
¼ cup dry white wine
3 to 4 scallions, thinly sliced
1 6- or 7-ounce jar roasted red bell peppers, drained and cut into ½-inch squares
½ cup reduced-fat sour cream
½ to 1 cup low-fat milk, as needed
Salt and freshly ground pepper to taste

Preheat the oven to 350 degrees, or a toaster oven to 375 degrees. Place the whole head or heads of garlic on a baking sheet and bake for 40 minutes.

Heat the oil in a soup pot. Add the onion and sauté over medium heat until golden. Add the potatoes, apple, and wine, and just enough water to cover. Bring to a simmer, then simmer gently, covered, for 35 to 40 minutes, until the potato is quite soft.

When the garlic is done, squeeze the soft pulp from the cloves right into the soup and discard the skins. Mash the potatoes in the soup with a potato masher until the base is thick and chunky.

Add the remaining ingredients, stir well, and let the soup stand off the heat for an hour before serving. Heat through very gently; don't allow the soup to come to a boil.

| Calories: 221 | Total fat: 4 g | Protein: 3 g |
| Carbohydrate: 40 g | Cholesterol: 2 g | Sodium: 32 mg |

Top with Cheddar.

Potato, Cheese, and Green Chili Soup

9-15

6 to 8 servings

This flavorful soup is a contemporary classic from the American Southwest. A great soup to make in the early fall, while fresh corn and tomatoes are still available.

5 medium potatoes, peeled and diced
5 cups Light Vegetable Stock (page 7) or water
1 tablespoon canola or olive oil
1 large onion, chopped
2 to 3 cloves garlic, crushed or minced
1 large green bell pepper, finely chopped
1 cup chopped fresh, ripe tomatoes (substitute canned if good, ripe tomatoes are unavailable)
1 cup cooked fresh or thawed frozen corn kernels
1 4-ounce can chopped mild green chilies
1 teaspoon chili powder
8 ounces reduced-fat cheddar cheese or cheddar-style soy cheese, grated
Salt and freshly ground pepper to taste

Place the potato dice in a soup pot and cover with the stock or water. Bring to a simmer, then simmer gently, covered, until the potatoes are just tender, about 15 minutes.

In the meantime, heat the oil in a small skillet. Sauté the onion over medium heat until it is translucent. Add the garlic and green pepper and sauté until the mixture begins to brown lightly.

Remove half of the potatoes from their cooking liquid with a slotted spoon and place them in a shallow bowl. Mash them well, then stir back into the soup pot, followed by the onion–bell pepper mixture. Add the tomatoes, corn, green chilies, and chili powder. Add additional water if the soup is too dense. Stir together, return to a simmer, then simmer gently for 20 minutes.

Sprinkle in the grated cheese, a little at a time, stirring it until it is fairly well melted each time (soy cheese may not melt as completely). Season to taste with salt and pepper and allow the soup to simmer over very low heat, stirring frequently, for another 5 minutes.

Serve at once, or let stand for an hour or so before serving. Heat through as needed and adjust the consistency with more water if the soup becomes too thick.

Calories: 269	Total fat: 8 g	Protein: 12 g
Carbohydrate: 35 g	Cholesterol: 23 g	Sodium: 260 mg

Sweet Potato Soup

6 servings

A warming soup with an appealing golden color. The natural sweetness of the sweet potatoes gives this soup a surprising flavor twist.

2 tablespoons soy margarine or canola oil
2 medium onions, chopped
2 medium carrots, peeled and diced
1 large celery stalk, diced
Handful of celery leaves
6 cups peeled, diced (about ½ inch)
    sweet potatoes
2 bay leaves
¼ teaspoon dried thyme
¼ teaspoon ground nutmeg
1 cup low-fat milk or soy milk, or as needed
Salt and freshly ground pepper to taste

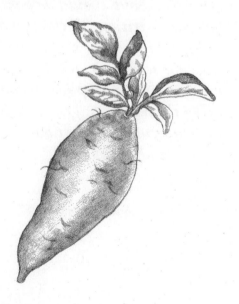

Heat the margarine or oil in a soup pot. Add the onion, carrots, and celery and sauté over low heat until the onions are golden. Add the celery leaves and sweet potato dice. Add just enough water to cover all but about an inch of the vegetables. Bring to a simmer, then stir in the bay leaves and seasonings. Simmer gently, covered, until the sweet potatoes and vegetables are quite tender, about 20 to 25 minutes.

With a slotted spoon, remove about half of the solid ingredients and transfer to a food processor along with about ½ cup of the cooking liquid. Process until smoothly pureed, then stir back into the soup pot. Add the milk or soy milk as needed to achieve a slightly thick consistency. Season to taste with salt and pepper. Simmer over very low heat for another 10 to 15 minutes.

Serve at once, or let stand off the heat for an hour or two before serving, then heat through as needed.

| Calories: 235 | Total fat: 5 g | Protein: 4 g |
| Carbohydrate: 46 g | Cholesterol: 2 g | Sodium: 96 mg |

Hot Beet and Potato Borscht

6 to 8 servings

Though beet borscht is generally eaten cold, the addition of potatoes creates a more robust version for fall or winter. Onion-Rye Oven Scones (page 145) complement this soup well.

1½ tablespoons canola oil
2 large onions, chopped
3 medium potatoes, peeled and grated
4 medium beets, peeled and grated
1 large carrot, peeled and grated
1 medium celery stalk, finely diced
Handful of celery leaves
1 cup fresh orange juice
Juice of 1 lemon
2 tablespoons minced fresh dill
    or 2 teaspoons dried dill
1 teaspoon dry mustard
Salt and freshly ground pepper to taste
Low-fat sour cream or plain low-fat yogurt,
    optional

Heat the oil in a soup pot. Add the onion and sauté over medium heat until golden. Add all the remaining ingredients except the salt and pepper and sour cream or yogurt. Add enough water to cover the vegetables, bring to a simmer, then simmer gently, covered, until the vegetables are tender, about 40 to 45 minutes. Adjust the consistency with more water if the soup is crowded. Season to taste with salt and pepper.

Allow the soup to stand for an hour or two before serving, then heat through as needed.

Garnish each serving with a small scoop of sour cream or yogurt if desired.

Calories: 121	Total fat: 3 g	Protein: 2 g
Carbohydrate: 22 g	Cholesterol: 0 g	Sodium: 28 mg

To be a maker of good soups one must not only have skill and patience, but must also use good materials....Soup should be palatable and nutritious. If these qualities be lacking, there will be no excuse for serving it. Knowledge and care must be applied in combining the various ingredients in order to secure results at once pleasing and healthful.

—Maria Parloa
Miss Parloa's Kitchen Companion, 1887

Curried Red Lentil Soup with Sweet Potatoes and Greens

6 servings

Both nourishing and sublimely satisfying, this thick soup incorporates fall's first sweet potatoes with seasonal greens. Red lentils, which cook to a warm golden color, are available in specialty food shops as well as natural food stores. Serve with Chapatis (page 148) or a store-bought flatbread.

2 tablespoons canola oil or soy margarine
1 cup chopped red onion
2 cloves garlic, minced
6 cups water
1½ cups red lentils, rinsed
2 large or 3 medium sweet potatoes, peeled and diced
1 teaspoon grated fresh ginger
2 teaspoons good quality curry powder or garam masala, more or less to taste
½ teaspoon ground coriander
¼ teaspoon each cinnamon and nutmeg
1 6-ounce bunch Swiss chard, escarole, or mustard greens
Juice of 1 lime
Salt to taste

Heat the oil or margarine in a soup pot. Add the onion and garlic and sauté over medium heat until golden brown, about 10 minutes. Add the water, lentils, sweet potatoes, and seasonings. Bring to a simmer, then simmer gently, covered, until the lentils are mushy and the potatoes are done, about 20 to 25 minutes.

In the meantime, wash the greens, remove their thick mid-ribs, then slice them into narrow shreds about 2 inches long. Stir into the soup along with the lime juice. If the soup is too thick, adjust the consistency with a small amount of water.

Continue to simmer gently until the greens are just done, about 10 to 15 minutes. Season to taste with salt. Serve at once, or let the soup stand for an hour or two, then heat through as needed.

Calories: 199   Total fat: 5 g   Protein: 8 g
Carbohydrate: 33 g   Cholesterol: 0 g   Sodium: 111 mg

Kale, Yellow Squash, and Sweet Potato Stew

6 to 8 servings

Kale is a sturdy member of the greens family with earthy flavored, elaborately ruffled leaves. As everyone knows, greens are good for you, but with its high calcium content, kale is a standout. Unlike many greens, kale does not wilt on contact with heat, but needs a good bit of simmering to get done. Its deep green color, contrasted with the yellow of the squash and the orange of the sweet potato, makes this an attractive and nourishing dish for the early autumn harvest.

1²/₃ cups water

²/₃ cup short or medium-grain brown rice, rinsed

1 tablespoon olive oil

1 medium-large red onion, chopped

2 cloves garlic, minced

6 ounces fresh kale

2 to 3 medium sweet potatoes, peeled and diced

5 cups Light Vegetable Stock (page 7) or 5 cups water with 1 vegetable bouillon cube

½ teaspoon grated fresh ginger

1 teaspoon dry mustard

2 small yellow summer squashes, diced

2 medium ripe tomatoes, diced

2 tablespoons soy sauce or tamari, or to taste

Freshly ground pepper to taste

Grated reduced-fat cheddar cheese or cheddar-style soy cheese for topping, optional

Bring the water to a boil in a small saucepan. Stir in the rice, cover, and simmer gently until done, about 35 minutes. In the meantime, heat the oil in a soup pot. Add the onion and garlic and sauté over medium heat until softened, about 10 minutes.

Cut the kale leaves away from the mid-ribs. Discard the mid-ribs. Chop the kale into bite-sized pieces and rinse well in a colander. Add to the soup pot along with the sweet potatoes and cover with the stock or water. Add the ginger and mustard and stir well. Bring to a simmer, then simmer gently, covered, for about 10 minutes.

Stir in the squash and tomatoes and simmer until the kale and sweet potato dice are tender, about 15 to 20 minutes. Mash enough of the sweet potato dice with the back of a wooden spoon to thicken the base. Season to taste with soy sauce or tamari and pepper. If time allows, let the stew stand for an hour or two before serving, then heat through as needed.

Top each serving with a sprinkling of grated cheese if desired.

Calories: 206	Total fat: 1 g	Protein: 4 g
Carbohydrate: 41 g	Cholesterol: 0 g	Sodium: 327 mg

Orange-Butternut Squash Soup *OK*

10-15

6 servings

A cheerfully colored soup with a hint of sweetness and the surprising crunch of water chestnuts. One you've got the squash baked, the rest is a snap.

1 large butternut squash
1 cup freshly squeezed orange juice
2 cups Light Vegetable Stock (page 7) or
    2 cups water with 1 vegetable
    bouillon cube
2 cups frozen green peas, thawed — *Spinach*
1 6- to 8-ounce can water chestnuts,
    finely diced
3 scallions, thinly sliced
1 teaspoon good quality curry powder or
    garam masala
¼ teaspoon ground ginger
¼ teaspoon cinnamon
Salt to taste

Preheat the oven to 375 degrees.

Halve the squash lengthwise and scrape out the seeds and fibers. Place the halves cut side up in a shallow baking dish and cover with foil. Bake for 45 to 50 minutes, or until soft. This step may be done ahead of time.

When the squash is cool enough to handle, scoop the flesh away from the peel and transfer to a food processor. Add the orange juice and puree until very smooth.

Transfer to a soup pot and add the stock or water. Stir together. Bring to a gentle simmer, then add the remaining ingredients. Cook, covered, for 10 minutes over medium-low heat.

Let the soup stand off the heat for 1 to 2 hours. Adjust the consistency, if needed, with more stock or water. The soup should have a thick but flowing consistency. Heat through as needed and serve.

| Calories: 107 | Total fat: 0 g | Protein: 3 g |
| Carbohydrate: 23 g | Cholesterol: 0 g | Sodium: 25 mg |

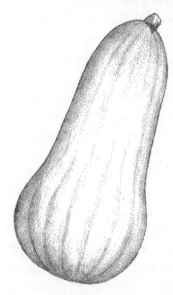

Spaghetti Squash Stew with Turnips and Snow Peas

8 servings

If it's possible for squash to be considered a "fun" food, I always find this to be true for spaghetti squash. It makes for a pleasantly offbeat stew ingredient.

1 medium spaghetti squash
2 tablespoons canola oil, divided
1 large onion, quartered and thinly sliced
2 cloves garlic, minced
1 28-ounce can diced tomatoes, undrained
¼ cup minced oil-cured sun-dried tomatoes
1 cup small mushrooms, thinly sliced
2 teaspoons salt-free herb-and-spice seasoning mix
½ teaspoon dried oregano
¼ teaspoon dried thyme
2 cups water
Salt and freshly ground pepper to taste
1 pound turnips, peeled and cut into thick matchsticks
2 cups snow peas, trimmed and cut in half lengthwise

Preheat the oven to 375 degrees.

Cut the squash in half lengthwise, then scrape out the seeds. Place the two halves, cut side up, in a shallow casserole dish filled with ½ inch of water. Cover tightly with foil and bake for 40 to 50 minutes, or until easily pierced with a fork.

When cool enough to handle, scrape the squash with a fork with long downward motions to remove the spaghetti-like strands.

Heat half of the oil in a soup pot. Add the onion and sauté over medium heat until translucent. Add the garlic and continue to sauté until the onion is golden and just beginning to brown. Add the spaghetti squash, tomatoes, sun-dried tomatoes, mushrooms, seasoning mix, and herbs, along with the water. Bring to a simmer, then simmer gently, covered, for 20 to 25 minutes. Season to taste with salt and pepper.

In the meantime, heat the remaining oil in a skillet. Add the turnips and sauté over medium-high heat, stirring frequently, until golden. Add the snow peas and continue to sauté, stirring, until the snow peas are bright green and crisp-tender.

Serve at once, topping each serving of the spaghetti squash stew with some of the turnips and snow peas.

| Calories: 102 | Total fat: 3 g | Protein: 3 g |
| Carbohydrate: 14 g | Cholesterol: 0 g | Sodium: 42 mg |

Gingered Pumpkin-Apple Soup

6 to 8 servings

Make this soup a day ahead, if you can. The unusual combination of flavors benefits from having time to blend.

1½ tablespoons soy margarine
1 large onion, finely chopped
2 medium celery stalks, finely diced
2 medium tart apples, peeled, cored, and diced
4 cups Light Vegetable Stock (page 7) or water
1 1-pound can unsweetened pumpkin puree
1 teaspoon grated fresh ginger
1 teaspoon good quality curry powder or garam masala
½ teaspoon cinnamon
¼ teaspoon nutmeg
2 cups low-fat milk or soy milk, or as needed
Salt to taste
Chopped toasted almonds or cashews for garnish, optional

Heat the margarine in a soup pot. Add the onion and celery and sauté over medium heat until the onion is golden. Add the remaining ingredients except for the last 3. Bring to a boil, then simmer over low heat, covered, for 35 to 40 minutes. Stir in enough milk or soy milk to achieve a smooth and slightly thick consistency. Season to taste with salt. Remove from heat.

Allow the soup to stand overnight or for several hours to develop flavor. Taste and add more seasonings if desired. Heat through as needed when ready to serve. Garnish each serving with a sprinkling of chopped almonds or cashews if desired.

Calories: 123	Total fat: 3 g	Protein: 4 g
Carbohydrate: 19 g	Cholesterol: 3 g	Sodium: 92 mg

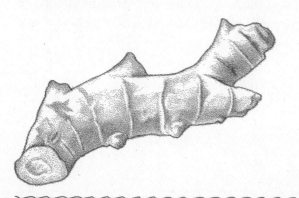

Moroccan-Style Vegetable Stew

6 or more servings

This delicious stew looks and smells as enticing as it tastes.

1½ tablespoons canola oil

2 large onions, chopped

2 medium potatoes, scrubbed and cut into ¾-inch chunks

2 heaping cups raw pumpkin or butternut squash, peeled and cut into ¾-inch chunks

2 large carrots, peeled and coarsely chopped

1 14-ounce can diced tomatoes, undrained

2 teaspoons ground cumin

¾ teaspoon turmeric

1 1-pound can chickpeas, drained and rinsed

Salt and freshly ground pepper to taste

1 cup raw couscous (see note)

2 cups boiling water

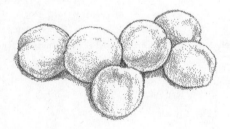

Heat the oil in a soup pot. Add the onions and sauté over moderate heat until golden. Add the potatoes, pumpkin or squash, carrots, tomatoes, and barely enough water to cover. Bring to a simmer, then add the seasonings and simmer gently, covered, for approximately 45 minutes, or until the vegetables are tender. Add the chickpeas, and season to taste with salt and pepper. Simmer over very low heat for another 15 minutes.

In the meantime, place the couscous in an ovenproof bowl. Cover with the boiling water, then cover the bowl and let stand for 15 minutes. Fluff with a fork. Place a small amount of the couscous in each soup bowl, then ladle the stew over it. Serve at once.

Note: Couscous is presteamed, cracked semolina, available in natural food stores and many supermarkets. You might like to try the whole grain variety, which is a soft tan color.

Calories: 317	Total fat: 4 g	Protein: 10 g
Carbohydrate: 57 g	Cholesterol: 0 g	Sodium: 31 mg

Squash and Corn Chower

6 to 8 servings

The perfect time to make this soup is early fall, when the first squash comes to the market and fresh corn is still being harvested.

1 medium butternut squash (about 1½ pounds)

2 tablespoons canola oil

1 heaping cup chopped onion

1 celery stalk, finely diced

1 large sweet potato, peeled and diced

Light Vegetable Stock (page 7) or water with 2 vegetable bouillon cubes, as needed

2 bay leaves

2 teaspoons salt-free herb-and-spice seasoning mix

½ teaspoon dried thyme

2½ to 3 cups cooked fresh corn kernels (from about 3 medium ears)

1 cup low-fat milk or soy milk, or as needed

Salt and freshly ground pepper to taste

With a sharp knife, cut the squash across the center of the rounded part. Remove the seeds and fibers. Slice the squash into ½-inch rings, then peel each ring and cut into small dice.

Heat the oil in a soup pot. Add the onion and celery and sauté over medium heat until the onion is golden. Add the squash and sweet potato dice and enough stock or water to cover all but about an inch of the vegetables. Bring to a simmer, then add the bay leaves and other seasonings. Simmer gently, covered, until the squash and potatoes are tender, about 25 to 30 minutes.

With a slotted spoon, scoop out 2 heaping cups of the solid ingredients, mash them well, and stir back into the soup. Add the cooked corn kernels and enough milk or soy milk to achieve a slightly thick consistency. Season to taste with salt and pepper. Simmer over low heat for another 10 to 15 minutes.

Serve at once, or let the soup stand for an hour or so before serving, then heat through as needed. This may also be cooked a day ahead and refrigerated, since its flavor develops nicely overnight.

| Calories: 178 | Total fat: 3 g | Protein: 4 g |
| Carbohydrate: 32 g | Cholestertol: 1 g | Sodium: 71 mg |

We dined on Indian corn and Squash soup, and boiled bread.

— John Bartram
Observations in His Travels, 1751

Southwestern Fresh Corn Stew

6 servings

While fresh local corn is abundant in early fall, the most tempting way to eat it is right off the cob. But cooking with fresh corn can be equally appealing. Its sweetness and crunch can't be matched by frozen corn kernels. Serve this with Savory Bean Bread (page 136) and a green salad for a hearty meal. Or, to vary the recipe, add a cup or two of cooked pinto or pink beans and serve with a purchased fresh bread.

1 tablespoon olive oil

1 large onion, chopped

2 to 3 cloves garlic, minced

4 medium ears fresh corn, kernels scraped from cob with a sharp knife

2 medium ripe tomatoes, diced

2 small yellow summer squashes, diced

1½ to 2 cups fresh green string beans, trimmed and cut into 1-inch lengths (see note)

1 14-ounce can pureed or crushed tomatoes

1 to 2 fresh chilies, seeded and minced, or 1 4-ounce can mild or medium-hot chopped chilies

1 to 1½ cups water

¼ cup finely chopped fresh cilantro or parsley

Salt and freshly ground pepper to taste

Reduced-fat sour cream, plain low-fat yogurt, or soy yogurt for topping, optional

Heat the oil in a soup pot. Add the onion and garlic and sauté over medium heat until the onion is golden. Add the corn kernels, tomatoes, squash, string beans, canned tomatoes, and chilies. Add enough water to make the mixture moist but not too soupy. Bring to a simmer, then simmer gently, covered, for 20 minutes.

Add the cilantro or parsley, then season to taste with salt and pepper. Simmer very gently for 5 to 10 minutes more, or until the corn kernels and squash are just tender. Serve in bowls topped with sour cream or yogurt if desired.

Note: If you can't find green beans that look fresh and tender, use frozen green beans. Thaw them and add them to the stew about 10 minutes after adding the other vegetables.

Calories: 186	Total fat: 2 g	Protein: 4 g
Carbohydrate: 36 g	Cholesterol: 0 g	Sodium: 43 mg

Never blow your soup if it is too hot, but wait until it cools.
Never raise your plate to your lips, but eat it with your spoon.

— C. B. Hartley
The Gentleman's Book of Etiquette, 1873

This gentleman eats his soup properly, but his posture is abominable, and his hat is on.

This gentleman's posture is excellent, but he eats his soup in a shockingly rude fashion.

Jerusalem Artichoke Puree with Leeks

6 to 8 servings

Jerusalem artichokes (sometimes marketed as "sunchokes") are a hardy fall root vegetable. Their offbeat flavor and texture, something of a cross between potatoes and water chestnuts, will appeal to adventurous soup-makers. Barley or Rice Triangles (page 142) complement this soup nicely.

1½ pounds Jerusalem artichokes,
    scrubbed and diced, divided
2 medium potatoes, peeled and diced
1 large onion, chopped
¼ cup white wine
½ teaspoon good quality curry powder
    or garam masala
Light Vegetable Stock (page 7) or
    water with 1 vegetable bouillon cube,
    as needed
2 large leeks
2 tablespoons canola oil
3 tablespoons minced fresh parsley
Juice of ½ lemon
Salt and freshly ground pepper to taste

Reserve and set aside about one third of the diced Jerusalem artichokes. Place the rest in a soup pot along with the potatoes, onion, wine, curry powder, and just enough stock or water to barely cover the vegetables. Bring to a simmer, then simmer gently, covered, until the vegetables are tender, about 20 minutes.

Transfer the soup to a food processor or blender and puree, in batches if necessary, until smooth. Return the puree to the soup pot. Add additional water or stock if the soup is too thick, just enough to achieve a smooth, medium-thick consistency. Return to low heat.

Cut the leeks into ¼-inch slices. Remove and discard the tough green leaves. Separate the rings of the leeks and rinse well to remove grit. Heat the oil in a skillet. Add the leeks and reserved artichoke dice and sauté over moderate heat until both are just beginning to brown lightly. Stir into the soup, along with the parsley and lemon juice, and season to taste with salt and pepper. If time allows, let the soup stand for an hour or so before serving, then heat through as needed.

Calories: 176	Total fat: 3 g	Protein: 3 g
Carbohydrate: 31 g	Cholesterol: 0 g	Sodium: 15 mg

Almond-Brussels Sprouts Soup

6 to 8 servings

Elegant and highly flavored, this soup features protein-rich almonds as its base. A fresh loaf of whole wheat bread and a salad of tomatoes and strong greens make excellent companions.

½ cup toasted almonds
1 tablespoon canola oil
1 large onion, chopped
1 large celery stalk, chopped
1 clove garlic, minced
1 large potato, peeled and diced
⅓ cup dry white wine
1 large tomato, diced
1½ pounds brussels sprouts, trimmed
   and coarsely chopped
2½ teaspoons salt-free herb-and-spice
   seasoning mix
1 to 2 tablespoons lemon juice, or to taste
Salt and freshly ground pepper to taste
Slivered or chopped almonds for garnish,
   optional
Chopped fresh parsley for garnish

Place the almonds in a food processor. Process until very finely ground. Continue to process until the mixture almost resembles a nut butter, stopping the machine and scraping down the sides with a plastic spatula from time to time.

Heat the oil in a soup pot. Add the onion and sauté over medium heat until it is golden.

Add the celery, garlic, potato, wine, tomato, and about two thirds of the brussels sprouts (reserve and set aside the remainder). Add enough water to barely cover the vegetables. Bring to a simmer, then add the almond butter and seasoning mix. Simmer gently, covered, over low heat for 35 to 40 minutes, or until all the vegetables are tender. Remove from the heat.

Transfer the solid ingredients to a food processor and puree, in batches if necessary, until smooth. Transfer back to the soup pot and return to low heat. Thin with a small amount of water if the soup is too thick.

In a separate saucepan, steam the reserved brussels sprouts in about ½ inch of water until they are bright green and crisp-tender. Add them to the soup along with lemon juice, and salt and pepper to taste. Serve the soup at once, or allow to stand for an hour or so before serving, then heat through as needed. Garnish each serving with some chopped or slivered almonds if desired and fresh parsley.

Calories: 164   Total fat: 8 g   Protein: 4 g
Carbohydrate: 16 g   Cholesterol: 0 g   Sodium: 31 mg

Chickpea and Tahini Soup

6 to 8 servings

The classic Middle Eastern team of chickpeas and tahini (sesame paste, available in natural food stores and Middle Eastern specialty groceries) is combined here in a tasty, offbeat soup. Serve with fresh whole wheat pita bread. The Middle Eastern bulgur salad, tabbouleh (recipes for which can be found in many vegetarian and Middle Eastern cookbooks), would round out this meal completely.

1 tablespoon olive oil

3 to 4 cloves garlic, minced

5 cups Light Vegetable Stock (page 7), **Onion or Leek and Garlic Broth (page 8), or cooking liquid from chickpeas**

2 cups mushrooms, coarsely chopped

1 cup finely shredded white cabbage

1 bay leaf

1 teaspoon ground cumin

2 teaspoons salt-free herb-and-spice seasoning mix

5 cups well-cooked or canned chickpeas (from about 1 pound dry chick-peas, or two 20-ounce cans), divided

¼ cup tahini (sesame paste)

¼ cup finely chopped fresh parsley

3 to 4 scallions, green parts only, thinly sliced

2 tablespoons minced fresh dill

Juice of ½ to 1 lemon, to taste

Salt and freshly ground pepper to taste

Heat the oil in a soup pot. Add the garlic and sauté over low heat for 1 minute. Add the stock, broth, or liquid, followed by the mushrooms, cabbage, bay leaf, and seasonings. Bring to a simmer, then simmer gently, covered, for 15 minutes.

In the meantime, set aside 1 cup of the chickpeas and place the remainder in a food processor or blender with the tahini. Process until very smoothly pureed. Stir the puree back into the liquid remaining in the soup pot.

Stir in the reserved chickpeas, bring to a simmer, then simmer very gently, covered, for 10 minutes. Add the remaining ingredients and adjust the consistency if necessary with more stock or water. Season to taste with salt and pepper, then simmer for another 10 minutes. Serve at once, or let stand for an hour or two before serving, then heat through as needed.

Calories: 275	Total fat: 8 g	Protein: 11 g
Carbohydrate: 37 g	Cholesterol: 0 g	Sodium: 13 mg

Chickpeas are under the dominion of Venus. They are less windy than beans, but nourish more...they have a cleansing facility.

— Nicolas Culpeper (1616 –1654)
  Culpeper's Complete Herbal

Broccoli, Apple, and Peanut Soup

6 to 8 servings

Peanut butter gives this soup an unusual, luscious flavor. Use reduced-fat peanut butter, now widely available in supermarkets, to reduce the fat impact!

1 tablespoon canola oil
2 tablespoons water
2 large onions, chopped
2 cloves garlic, minced
3 medium carrots, peeled and sliced, divided
6 cups Light Vegetable Stock (page 7) or water with 1 vegetable bouillon cube
¼ cup dry white wine
1 teaspoon good quality curry powder or garam masala
4 heaping cups finely chopped broccoli, divided
2 medium apples, peeled, cored, and diced
½ cup reduced-fat peanut butter
Juice of ½ lemon
Salt to taste
Chopped roasted peanuts for garnish, optional

Heat the oil and water slowly in a soup pot. Add the onions and garlic and sauté over medium heat until the onions are golden.

Set aside about one third of the carrot slices and about 1 heaping cup of broccoli florets. Place the remaining carrots in the soup pot along with the stock or water, wine, and curry powder or garam masala. Bring to a simmer, then simmer gently, covered, for 10 minutes. Add the broccoli and apple and continue to simmer until the carrots and broccoli are tender, about 10 minutes more. Remove from the heat.

Transfer the solid ingredients from the soup to a food processor or blender with a slotted spoon, about half at a time. Puree each batch with about half of the peanut butter. Stir the puree back into the soup stock in the pot. If the soup is too thick, add enough additional water or stock to achieve a medium-thick consistency. Return to low heat and simmer for 10 minutes.

In the meantime, steam the reserved carrots in a heavy saucepan with about ¼ cup water, covered, for 5 minutes. Add the reserved broccoli florets and steam for another 5 minutes, just until both are brightly colored and crisp-tender. Stir into the soup along with the lemon juice. Season to taste with salt and remove from the heat.

Garnish each serving with a handful of chopped peanuts if desired.

Calories: 232	Total fat: 11 g	Protein: 4 g
Carbohydrate: 22 g	Cholesterol: 0 g	Sodium: 131 mg

Swiss Chard Soup with Tortellini and Sun-Dried Tomatoes

8 or more servings

A bountiful and nourishing soup made special with the addition of tortellini.

⅔ cup sun-dried tomatoes (not oil cured)
1 cup hot water
1 tablespoon olive oil
1 medium onion, finely chopped
2 medium carrots, peeled and finely diced
1 large bunch Swiss chard (12 ounces to 1 pound)
6 cups water
1 14- to 16-ounce can diced tomatoes, undrained
12 ounces cheese-filled tortellini, regular or spinach
1½ teaspoons Italian herb mix
1 medium yellow summer squash, finely diced
2 tablespoons minced fresh dill or 1 teaspoon dried dill
Salt and freshly ground pepper to taste
Grated Parmesan cheese or soy Parmesan for topping, optional

Cover the dried tomatoes with the hot water in a small bowl. Let stand until needed.

Heat the oil in a large soup pot. Add the onion and carrot and sauté over medium heat, covered, stirring occasionally, until the onion is golden.

In the meantime, wash the Swiss chard, then trim the thick mid-ribs and cut into approximately ½-by-2-inch shreds. Place in another large pot and steam with just the water that clings to the leaves, covered, until limp and bright green, about 5 to 7 minutes. Remove from the heat.

Cover the onion and carrots in the soup pot with 6 cups of water, along with the tomatoes, tortellini, and Italian seasoning. Bring to a simmer, then simmer gently, covered, for 15 minutes. Add the yellow squash and the fresh or dried dill and simmer, covered, for another 10 minutes, or until the tortellini and the squash are done. Stir in the Swiss chard, add more water if the soup seems crowded, then season to taste with salt and pepper.

If time allows, let the soup stand for an hour or so before serving, then heat through as needed. Top each serving with a sprinkling of Parmesan cheese or soy Parmesan if desired.

Calories: 191	Total fat: 4 g	Protein: 8 g
Carbohydrate: 29 g	Cholesterol: 13 g	Sodium: 396 mg

Sauerkraut Soup

6 to 8 servings

An offbeat, pungent and sweet soup that takes the chill out of a nippy fall afternoon. Serve with Onion-Rye Oven Scones (page 145) or a purchased fresh rye bread.

1 tablespoon canola oil
1 large onion, quartered and thinly sliced
2 medium carrots, peeled and thinly sliced
1 large celery stalk, finely diced
6 cups water
2 medium apples, peeled and finely diced
1 1-pound can sauerkraut, drained
1 14- to 16-ounce can diced tomatoes, undrained
1 teaspoon salt-free herb-and-spice seasoning mix
¼ cup light brown sugar, more or less to taste
1 1-pound can small white beans, drained and rinsed
Freshly ground pepper to taste

Heat the oil in a soup pot. Add the onion and sauté over medium heat until golden. Add the carrots, celery, and water. Bring to a boil, then cover and simmer over moderate heat for 15 minutes.

Add the remaining ingredients and simmer for another 30 to 40 minutes, or until the carrots and celery are tender. Add more water if the soup seems crowded and adjust the seasonings. If time allows, let the soup stand off the heat for an hour or so before serving, then heat through as needed.

Calories: 201	Total fat: 2 g	Protein: 7 g
Carbohydrate: 38 g	Cholesterol: 0 g	Sodium: 476 mg

The Greeks hold that cabbage taken as a food greatly brightens the vision, and that the benefit is very great indeed if the juice of raw cabbage and Attic honey merely touch the corners of the eyes.

— Pliny the Elder
Pliny's Natural History, A.D. 1

Hot Slaw Soup

6 servings

This soup was inspired by the combination of ingredients used in the classic American salad. Cheddar-Oat Griddle Biscuits (page 143) or Cheese and Herb Corn Muffins (page 140) enhance this soup nicely.

1½ tablespoons canola oil

2 medium onions, grated or minced

4 cups grated or finely shredded white
    cabbage

2 medium carrots, peeled and grated

1 medium parsnip or white turnip, peeled
    and cut in ¼-inch dice

1 medium celery stalk, finely diced

Light Vegetable Stock (page 7) or water
    with 2 vegetable bouillon cubes, as
    needed

⅓ cup quick-cooking oats

2 teaspoons salt-free herb-and-spice
    seasoning mix

1 teaspoon dried dill

2 to 3 tablespoons apple cider vinegar,
    to taste

1½ to 2 cups low-fat milk or soy milk,
    as needed

Salt and freshly ground pepper to taste

Low-fat sour cream or plain low-fat
    yogurt, optional

Heat the oil in a large soup pot. Add the onions and sauté over medium heat until golden. Add the cabbage, carrots, parsnip or turnip, and celery along with just enough stock or water to cover. Bring to a simmer, then simmer gently, covered, until the vegetables are nearly tender, about 20 to 25 minutes. Stir in the oats, seasoning mix, dill, and vinegar, and simmer for another 10 to 15 minutes, or until the vegetables are done.

Stir in the milk or soy milk as needed, then season to taste with salt and pepper. Simmer just until the soup is heated through.

Serve at once, or let the soup stand for an hour or two before serving, then heat through as needed. If you like, top each serving with a small scoop of sour cream or yogurt.

Calories: 139	Total fat: 4 g	Protein: 5 g
Carbohydrate: 20 g	Cholesterol: 3 g	Sodium: 65 mg

Last night with the celery, autumn came into its own. There is a crispness about celery that is the essence of October. It is as fresh and clean as a rainy day after a spell of heat.

— A. A. Milne
  Not That It Matters, 1920

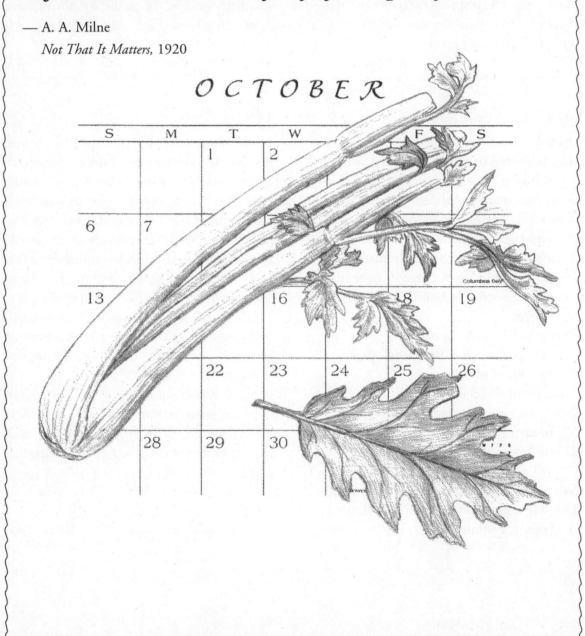

Garlicky Cream of Celery Soup

6 servings

This smooth soup will win you over with its elegant simplicity and intense celery flavor. Nothing enhances it better than Garlic Croutons (page 149).

12 large celery stalks, divided
2 tablespoons canola oil, divided
1 large onion, chopped
8 cloves garlic, minced
2 tablespoons unbleached white flour
3 medium potatoes, peeled and diced
2 teaspoons salt-free herb-and-spice
    seasoning mix
¼ cup mixed chopped fresh parsley
    and dill
¼ cup celery leaves
1 to 1½ cups low-fat milk or soy milk,
    as needed
Salt and freshly ground pepper to taste
Chopped fresh dill or parsley for garnish

Trim 10 stalks of celery and cut them into ½-inch dice. Trim the remaining 2 stalks, cut them into ¼-inch dice, and set aside.

Heat 1 tablespoon of the oil in a soup pot. Add the onions and garlic and sauté over medium heat until the onions are lightly golden. Sprinkle in the flour and stir it in until it disappears. Add the 10 stalks of celery, the potatoes, and just enough water to cover. Bring to a simmer, then add the seasoning mix, fresh herbs, and celery leaves. Simmer gently until the vegetables are tender, about 25 minutes. Remove from the heat.

With a slotted spoon, transfer the solid ingredients to a food processor or blender and puree, in batches if necessary, until very smooth. Stir back into the soup pot. Return to very low heat and add enough milk or soy milk to achieve a slightly thick consistency.

Heat the remaining oil in a small skillet. Add the reserved celery and sauté over moderate heat until it is touched with golden spots. Add to the soup, then season to taste with salt and pepper.

Serve at once, or allow the soup to stand for an hour or so, then heat through as needed. Garnish each serving with chopped dill or parsley.

Calories: 126	Total fat: 2 g	Protein: 3 g
Carbohydrate: 22 g	Cholesterol: 2 g	Sodium: 101 mg

Hot-and-Sour Oriental Vegetable Soup

6 servings

Don't be intimidated by the long list of ingredients here. It's an easy soup to make, doesn't take long to cook, and is full of exciting textures and flavors.

6 dried shiitake mushrooms
1 cup hot water
1 tablespoon canola or peanut oil
1 teaspoon dark sesame oil
1 medium onion, quartered and sliced
2 or 3 stalks bok choy or 2 large celery
   stalks, sliced diagonally
1 14- to 16-ounce can diced tomatoes,
   undrained
1 cup fresh white mushrooms, coarsely
   chopped
Liquid from the canned baby corn and
   water chestnuts, plus enough water to
   make 5 cups
1 teaspoon lemon-pepper
1 cup snow peas, cut into 1-inch pieces
1 6-ounce can water chestnuts, sliced,
   liquid reserved
1 16-ounce can baby corn, liquid reserved
3 to 5 tablespoons rice vinegar, to taste
Chili oil, cayenne pepper, or any hot
   sauce (such as Tabasco), to taste
2 tablespoons soy sauce
½ pound firm tofu, cut into ½-inch dice
2 scallions, minced
2 tablespoons cornstarch
¼ cup cold water

Place the dried mushrooms in a bowl to soak in the hot water and set aside until needed.

Heat the oils in a soup pot. Add the onion and sauté over low heat until golden. Add the bok choy or celery, tomatoes, white mushrooms, 5 cups liquid, and lemon-pepper. Bring to a simmer, then cook at a gentle simmer, covered, until the bok choy or celery is crisp-tender, about 10 minutes.

In the meantime, trim and discard the tough stems of the soaked dried mushrooms. Slice the caps. Add them with their soaking liquid to the soup, along with the remaining ingredients, except the cornstarch. Taste frequently as you add the vinegar and hot seasoning. Simmer over very low heat for 8 to 10 minutes.

Dissolve the cornstarch in the cold water. Slowly drizzle into the soup while stirring. Simmer over very low heat for another 5 minutes. Remove from the heat and serve at once.

| Calories: 187 | Total fat: 5 g | Protein: 6 g |
| Carbohydrate: 29 g | Cholesterol: 0 g | Sodium: 360 mg |

"Buddhist's Delight" Stew

6 to 8 servings

This medley of Oriental vegetables, inspired by my favorite Chinese restaurant fare, is enhanced with protein-packed seitan. Seitan, made from cooked wheat gluten, is sometimes called "wheat meat," as it bears a resemblance to beef chunks. Though dense and chewy and in a sense quite "meaty," seitan is very low in fat, and its grainy flavor will likely not put off those who don't care for meat. Seitan is available in many natural food stores, packed in a tasty broth in the same type of sealed tubs in which tofu is often sold. You can also buy an excellent seitan "quick mix" and make it yourself.

1 pound fresh seitan, broth reserved
1 large bunch broccoli, cut into bite-sized pieces
2 cups fresh green beans, trimmed and cut into 1-inch pieces
3 large carrots, peeled and sliced diagonally
2 cloves garlic, minced
1 recipe Oriental Mushroom Broth (page 11) with trimmed shiitake mushrooms
1½ cups small white mushrooms
1 1-pound can baby corn, drained (reserve liquid for another use)
4 ounces rice-stick noodles (see note)
¼ cup cornstarch
3 tablespoons soy sauce or tamari, or to taste

Drain the broth from the seitan (about ¾ to 1 cup) into a soup pot or large steep-sided wok. Cut the seitan into bite-sized chunks and set aside. Add the broccoli, green beans, carrots, and garlic to the broth in the pot. Bring to a gentle boil, then cover and cook for 3 to 5 minutes, until the broccoli and green beans are bright green.

Add the Oriental Mushroom Broth, seitan, shiitake and white mushrooms, baby corn, and rice-stick noodles. Bring to a simmer and cook over medium-high heat, uncovered, until the noodles are done and the vegetables are crisp-tender, about 8 to 10 minutes.

Put the cornstarch in a small bowl or mixing cup and stir in just enough of the liquid from the soup pot to smoothly dissolve it. Slowly pour into the soup pot and simmer just until the broth has thickened up. Serve at once.

Note: Rice-stick noodles are also available in natural food stores, as well as Asian groceries.

Calories: 270	Total fat: 5 g	Protein: 24 g
Carbohydrate: 162 g	Cholesterol: 0 g	Sodium: 284 mg

Black Bean Soup

6 to 8 servings

A classic American soup, this is robust and brimming with complex flavors. With any of the muffins, pages 139 to 141, and a simple salad, this soup is the basis of a filling and hearty meal.

1 pound dried black (turtle) beans
1 cup chopped onion
2 large carrots, peeled and chopped
2 large celery stalks, diced
2 or 3 cloves garlic, crushed or minced
3 tablespoons chopped fresh parsley
2 bay leaves
2 teaspoons salt-free herb-and-spice
   seasoning mix
¼ teaspoon nutmeg
¼ cup dry red wine or sherry
Salt and freshly ground pepper to taste

Garnish:
1 tablespoon canola or light olive oil
1 large onion, quartered and thinly sliced
1 lemon, thinly sliced
Finely chopped fresh parsley

Rinse and sort the beans, discarding withered ones and checking carefully for small stones. Soak overnight in plenty of water, or cover with water, bring to a boil, then let stand off the heat for an hour.

Drain the beans and rinse. Place in a soup pot with fresh water in a ratio of approximately 3 parts water to 1 part beans. Bring to a simmer, then cover and simmer steadily for 1 hour. Add the onion, carrots, celery, garlic, parsley, bay leaves, seasoning mix, nutmeg, and wine or sherry. Simmer for another 1 to 1 ½ hours, or until the beans are soft.

Scoop out about 1 ½ cups of the beans with a slotted spoon, avoiding as much as possible scooping out the other vegetables. Set aside.

Discard the bay leaves and transfer the solid ingredients, in batches, to a food processor or blender. Use about ¼ cup cooking liquid per batch. Process until smoothly pureed, then return the puree to the soup pot along with the reserved beans. Season to taste with salt and pepper and return to low heat for 15 minutes.

Just before serving, heat the oil in a small skillet. Add the sliced onion and sauté over medium heat until golden brown.

Garnish each serving with some of the sautéed onion, 2 lemon slices, and some chopped parsley. This soup keeps very well for several days, and the flavor improves as it stands.

Calories: 217	Total fat: 2 g	Protein: 10 g
Carbohydrate: 36 g	Cholesterol: 0 g	Sodium: 25 mg

Beans possess over all vegetables the great advantage of being just as good, if not better, when kept waiting, an advantage in the case of people whose disposition or occupation makes it difficult for them to be punctual.

— André Simon

The Concise Dictionary of Gastronomy, 1952

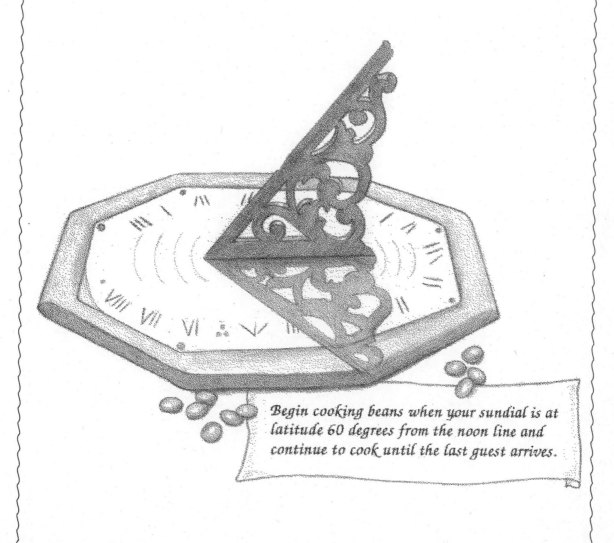

Begin cooking beans when your sundial is at latitude 60 degrees from the noon line and continue to cook until the last guest arrives.

W·I·N·T·E·R

Winter is the very best time for soup — nothing offers better comfort to body and soul when coming in from the cold. What a perfect time to make thick soups of grains and legumes. Teamed with bread and salad, most of the soups in this section make satisfying meals in and of themselves.

cold front

Minestrone

8 or more servings

Filling and tasty, this Italian vegetable soup becomes a meal in itself when served with a robust bread such as Focaccia Bread (page 138). It keeps exceptionally well and develops flavor as it stands.

2 tablespoons olive oil
2 medium onions, finely chopped
2 cloves garlic, minced
2 medium carrots, peeled and diced
2 medium celery stalks, diced
Handful of celery leaves, chopped
2 medium potatoes, peeled and diced
2 cups shredded white cabbage
1 14- to 16-ounce can diced tomatoes, undrained
1 cup tomato sauce
¼ cup dry red wine, optional
2 bay leaves
2 teaspoons Italian herb mix
1 1-pound can chickpeas, drained and rinsed
1 cup frozen green peas, thawed
2 tablespoons minced fresh parsley
Salt and freshly ground pepper to taste

Heat the oil in a soup pot. Add the onions and garlic and sauté over moderate heat until the onions are golden. Add the carrots, celery, celery leaves, potatoes, and cabbage, along with just enough water to cover. Add the tomatoes, tomato sauce, optional wine, bay leaves, and seasoning mix.

Bring to a simmer, then simmer gently, covered, until the vegetables are just done, about 45 minutes. Add the chickpeas, green peas, and parsley. Correct the consistency with more water if necessary, then season to taste with salt and pepper. Simmer over low heat for at least another 20 to 30 minutes, or until the vegetables are completely tender but not overdone.

Calories: 187
Total fat: 5 g
Protein: 6 g
Carbohydrate: 31 g
Cholesterol: 0 g
Sodium: 217 mg

Italian Pasta and Bean Soup

8 or more servings

Like Minestrone, this is an Italian standard. Serve it with Parmesan Pita Wedges (page 148) or Bruschetta (page 150).

2 tablespoons extra-virgin olive oil
1 medium onion, finely chopped
2 cloves garlic, minced
1 medium carrot, peeled and cut into
   ¼-inch dice
1 large celery stalk, cut into ¼-inch dice
4 cups cooked or canned Great Northern
   beans (cannellini), from about 1½
   cups raw, or 2 1-pound cans,
   drained and rinsed
7 cups cooking liquid from beans,
   or water
2 cups diced zucchini
2 bay leaves
1½ teaspoons Italian herb mix
¼ cup tomato paste
1½ cups ditalini (tiny tubular pasta)
2 tablespoons chopped fresh parsley
Salt and freshly ground pepper to taste

Heat the olive oil in a soup pot. Add the onion, garlic, carrot, and celery, and sauté over medium heat, stirring frequently, until the onion is golden. Add the beans, cooking liquid or water, zucchini, bay leaves, herb mix, and tomato paste. Bring to a simmer, then simmer gently, covered, until the zucchini is just tender, about 10 minutes. Remove from the heat and allow the soup to stand for an hour or so to develop flavor.

In a separate saucepan, cook the pasta al dente. Rinse briefly under cool water until it stops steaming. Add the parsley to the soup and heat it through. When the soup is hot, add the cooked pasta and season to taste with salt and pepper. Serve at once.

| Calories: 234 | Total fat: 5 g | Protein: 10 g |
| Carbohydrate: 40 g | Cholesterol: 0 g | Sodium: 19 mg |

Italian Vegetable Stew with Gnocchi

8 or more servings

Gnocchi are dumplings made of semolina and potato flours. They add a special touch to this flavorful vegetable stew. They are available at many supermarkets, found in the frozen food section near the frozen ravioli, tortellini, and other such Italian specialties.

2 tablespoons olive oil
1 large onion, chopped
3 cloves garlic, minced
2 cups thinly shredded white cabbage
2 medium potatoes, peeled and diced
1 to 1½ cups fresh string beans, cut into 1-inch lengths
1 14- to 16-ounce can diced tomatoes, undrained
1 14- to 16-ounce can pureed or crushed tomatoes
¼ cup dry red wine
1 teaspoon Italian herb mix
½ teaspoon dried basil
3 heaping cups cauliflower, cut into bite-sized pieces
1 medium zucchini, quartered lengthwise and sliced
1 pound frozen gnocchi, thawed
Salt and freshly ground pepper to taste
¼ cup chopped fresh parsley
Grated Parmesan cheese or soy Parmesan for topping, optional

Heat the oil in a soup pot. Add the onion, garlic, and cabbage and sauté over medium heat, covered, lifting the lid to stir occasionally, about 10 minutes. The vegetables should be limp and just beginning to turn golden.

Add the potatoes, string beans, tomatoes, tomato puree, wine, and seasonings, along with the water. Bring to a simmer, then simmer gently, covered, until the vegetables are just tender, about 15 minutes. Add the cauliflower and zucchini and cook for another 10 to 15 minutes, until all the vegetables are done but not overcooked.

In the meantime, cook the gnocchi separately in a large pot according to package directions. Most prepared gnocchi are cooked in approximately 10 minutes. When done, drain and gently stir into the stew. Season to taste with salt and pepper and stir in the parsley. The stew should have a thick, moist base, but not be too soupy. Add a bit more water if needed.

Serve the stew at once, or, if time allows, let it stand off the heat for an hour or two before serving, then heat through as needed. If you'd like, top each serving with grated Parmesan cheese or soy Parmesan.

Calories: 252	Total fat: 8 g	Protein: 6 g
Carbohydrate: 36 g	Cholesterol: 27 g	Sodium: 94 mg

The making of a good soup is quite an art, and many otherwise clever cooks do not possess the tour de main *necessary to its successful preparation. Either they over-complicate the composition of the dish, or they attach only minor importance to it, reserving their talents for the meal itself, and so it frequently happens that the soup does not correspond to the quality of the rest of the dishes; nevertheless, the quality of the soup should foretell that of the entire meal.*

— Madame Seignobos
  Comment on forme une cuisinière, 1903

Macaroni and Cheese Soup

6 to 8 servings

A smooth, mild soup, this melds pureed white beans with cheese and pasta for a high-protein result.

1½ tablespoons soy margarine or canola oil
1 large onion, finely chopped
2 medium celery stalks, finely diced
1 1-pound can Great Northern beans (cannellini), drained and rinsed
3½ cups Light Vegetable Stock (page 7) or water
½ pound mushrooms, coarsely chopped
1½ teaspoons salt-free herb-and-spice seasoning mix
1 cup low-fat milk or soy milk, or as needed
1½ cups firmly packed grated reduced-fat cheddar cheese or cheddar-style soy cheese
2 cups small pasta, such as shells or elbows
Salt to taste
Dash cayenne pepper

Heat the margarine or oil in a soup pot. Add the onion and celery and sauté over medium low heat until the onion is golden.

In the meantime, puree the beans in a blender or food processor until smooth. Add a small amount of water if necessary.

Cover the onions and celery with the stock or water. Bring to a simmer, then stir in the bean puree, mushrooms, and seasoning mix. Simmer gently, covered, for 30 to 35 minutes. Stir in the milk or soy milk, more or less as needed to achieve a slightly thick consistency. Remove from the heat and sprinkle in the cheese, a bit at a time, stirring in each time until it is fairly well melted (soy cheese may not melt as completely). Cover the soup and set aside.

In a separate saucepan, cook the pasta al dente. Drain it and stir into the soup. Adjust the consistency of the soup with more milk or soy milk, if needed, then return to low heat. Season to taste with salt and cayenne. Remove the soup from the heat once it is heated through and serve.

| Calories: 322 | Total fat: 8 g | Protein 16 g |
| Carbohydrate: 43 g | Cholesterol: 19 g | Sodium: 244 mg |

Dilled Potato, Pink Bean, and Green Bean Soup

6 servings

Both soothing and lively, thanks to the flavor of dill (do try to use fresh if you can), this simple soup is one of my winter favorites.

1 tablespoon olive oil
1 medium onion, finely chopped
2 cloves garlic, minced
4 medium potatoes, scrubbed and diced
1 28-ounce can diced or stewed tomatoes
¼ cup dry white wine
1 teaspoon each ground cumin, paprika, and salt-free herb-and-spice seasoning mix
1-pound can pink beans, drained and rinsed
2 cups frozen cut green beans, thawed
2 tablespoons minced fresh dill (or more to taste) or 2 teaspoons dried dill
¼ cup chopped fresh parsley
Salt and freshly ground pepper to taste

Heat the olive oil in a soup pot. Add the onion and garlic and sauté over medium heat for 5 minutes. Add the diced potatoes with just enough water to cover, followed by the tomatoes, wine, and spices. Bring to a simmer, then simmer gently, covered, until the potatoes are just done, about 20 minutes.

Add the pink beans and green beans. If not using fresh dill, add the dried at this point. Cook over low heat for another 20 to 25 minutes. Stir in the fresh herbs and season to taste with salt and pepper. Serve at once, or let the soup stand off the heat for an hour or two, then heat through as needed.

| Calories: 226 | Total fat: 2 g | Protein: 7 g |
| Carbohydrate: 42 g | Cholesterol: 0 g | Sodium: 21 mg |

Winter Celery, Potato, and Mushroom Soup

6 servings

This is just the sort of mild soup that is so comforting on cold winter days. Quick Sunflower-Cheese Bread (page 134) is a good accompaniment, as are Cheddar-Oat Griddle Biscuits (page 143).

2 tablespoons canola oil
1 large or 2 medium onions, chopped
2 tablespoons unbleached white flour
5 cups Light Vegetable Stock (page 7) or
    water with 2 vegetable bouillon cubes
4 large celery stalks, diced
Handful of celery leaves
3 medium potatoes, diced
⅓ cup raw pearl or pot barley, rinsed
2 bay leaves
½ pound coarsely chopped mushrooms
2 teaspoons salt-free herb-and-spice
    seasoning mix
1 cup frozen green peas, thawed
1½ to 2 cups low-fat milk or soy milk,
    or as needed
Salt and freshly ground pepper to taste

Heat the oil in a soup pot. Add the onions and sauté over medium heat until golden. Sprinkle in the flour a bit at a time and stir in until it disappears. Slowly pour in the stock or water, then add the celery, celery leaves, potatoes, barley, and bay leaves. Bring to a simmer, then simmer gently, covered, for 15 minutes.

Add the mushrooms and seasoning mix and simmer until the barley is tender, another 25 to 30 minutes. Add the green peas and enough milk or soy milk to achieve a medium-thick consistency. Season to taste with salt and pepper and simmer over very low heat for another 10 minutes.

This soup thickens as it stands; thin any leftovers with additional milk or soy milk, then taste to correct the seasonings.

Calories: 251	Total fat: 6 g	Protein: 7 g
Carbohydrate: 42 g	Cholesterol: 3 g	Sodium: 88 mg

Creamy Parsnip-Vegetable Soup

6 servings

This soothing winter soup is surprisingly elegant, especially if served with any of the dumplings on pages 151 to 153.

1½ tablespoons canola oil

1½ cups chopped onion

1 large celery stalk, diced

Handful of celery leaves

1 pound parsnips, scraped and cut into ½-inch dice

2 large potatoes, peeled and cut into ½-inch dice

2 medium carrots, peeled and coarsely chopped

1 14- to 16-ounce can diced tomatoes, undrained

1½ teaspoons salt-free herb-and-spice seasoning mix

2 tablespoons minced fresh parsley

1½ to 2 cups whole milk or soy milk, as needed

Salt and freshly ground pepper to taste

Heat the oil in a soup pot. Add the onion and celery and sauté over medium heat until the onion is golden. Add the celery leaves, parsnips, potatoes, carrots, tomatoes, seasoning mix, and just enough water to cover. Bring to a simmer, then simmer gently, covered, until the vegetables are tender, about 20 to 30 minutes. Remove from the heat.

With a slotted spoon, transfer half of the vegetables to a food processor or blender. Process until smoothly pureed, then stir back into the soup. Stir in the parsley and enough milk or soy milk to achieve a slightly thick consistency. Season to taste with salt and pepper. Return the soup to very low heat for 10 to 15 minutes — do not let it boil — then serve.

This soup thickens as it cools. Adjust the consistency of any leftover soup with additional water, milk, or soy milk, and taste to correct the seasonings.

Parsnip dressed in creame...will fatten exceedingly; but it ingenders lust and longing desires.

— William Vaughn
Directions for Health, 1600

| Calories: 208 | Total fat: 6 g | Protein: 5 g |
| Carbohydrate: 34 g | Cholesterol: 10 g | Sodium: 70 mg |

Hearty Winter Roots Soup

6 to 8 servings

As with the previous recipe, any of the dumplings on pages 151 to 153 are highly compatible with this satisfying soup.

2 tablespoons canola oil
1 large onion, chopped
2 cups peeled, diced rutabaga
2 medium carrots, peeled and coarsely
   chopped
2 medium potatoes, scrubbed and diced
2 medium parsnips, diced
1 large celery stalk, diced
⅓ cup rolled oats, rolled wheat, or
   rolled rye
¼ cup dry white wine
2 teaspoons salt-free herb-and-spice
   seasoning mix
1½ cups low-fat milk or soy milk,
   or as needed
1 cup grated reduced-fat cheddar cheese
   or cheddar-style soy cheese
Salt and freshly ground pepper to taste

Heat the oil in a soup pot. Add the onion and sauté over medium heat until golden. Add the vegetables along with just enough water to cover. Add all the remaining ingredients except the last 3 and stir together well. Bring to a simmer, then simmer gently, covered, until the vegetables are tender, about 30 to 40 minutes.

With a slotted spoon, remove about 2 cups of the vegetables and mash coarsely, then stir back into the soup. Add the milk or soy milk and allow the soup to simmer over very low heat for another 10 minutes.

Sprinkle in the cheese, a little at a time, stirring it in until fairly well melted each time (soy cheese may not melt as completely). If the soup is too thick, adjust the consistency with a bit more milk or soy milk, then season to taste with salt and pepper. If time allows, let the soup stand for an hour or so before serving, then heat through slowly, over low heat, as needed.

| Calories: 231 | Total fat 8 g | Protein: 9 g |
| Carbohydrate: 29 g | Cholesterol: 14 g | Sodium: 173 mg |

Creamy Carrot Bisque

3-18
neh.

6 to 8 servings

This pretty, pale orange soup gets substance from a base of pureed tofu.

1 pound carrots, peeled and sliced

3 medium turnips, peeled and diced, divided

1 medium onion, chopped

2 bay leaves

2 teaspoons salt-free herb-and-spice seasoning mix

1 cup crumbled soft or silken tofu

1 14-ounce can Italian plum tomatoes, undrained

¼ teaspoon each ground ginger and cinnamon

2 teaspoons canola oil

3 scallions, sliced

1 cup frozen green peas, thawed

2 to 3 tablespoons finely chopped fresh parsley

½ cup orange juice

Salt and freshly ground pepper to taste

In a large soup pot, combine the carrots, about two thirds of the diced turnips (set aside the rest), the onion, bay leaves, and seasoning mix. Add just enough water to cover, bring to a simmer, and cook, covered, for 25 to 30 minutes, or until the vegetables are tender. Remove from the heat. Remove and discard the bay leaves.

With a slotted spoon, transfer the vegetables to a food processor or blender. Process until smoothly pureed, then transfer back to the soup pot.

Combine the tofu and tomatoes in the food processor or blender. Process until smoothly pureed and transfer into the soup pot. Stir until both purees are well integrated and return to medium heat. Stir in the ginger and cinnamon.

Heat the oil in a small skillet. Add the reserved turnip dice and sauté over medium heat until crisp-tender and golden, stirring frequently. Add the scallions and sauté another minute or two, just until they are wilted. Remove from the heat and transfer the mixture to the soup, along with the peas and parsley.

Add the orange juice and season to taste with salt and pepper. The soup should have a smooth, medium-thick consistency. Add a bit more juice or water if necessary. Simmer very gently over very low heat for another 15 minutes. If time allows, let the soup stand off the heat for an hour or two before serving, then heat through as needed.

Calories: 114   Total fat: 2 g   Protein: 5 g
Carbohydrate: 18 g   Cholesterol: 0 g   Sodium: 87 mg

Sweet-and Sour Cabbage and Bread Stew

Serves 6

A hearty variation on sweet-and-sour cabbage soup, a great cold-weather classic.

2 tablespoons canola oil
2 large onions, quartered and thinly sliced
3 to 4 cloves garlic
2 large carrots, peeled and diced
2 large or 3 medium potatoes, diced
4 cups coarsely shredded green cabbage
1 medium green or red bell pepper, diced
1 14- to 16-ounce can diced or stewed
    tomatoes, undrained
¼ cup dry red wine
1 teaspoon paprika
½ teaspoon cumin
5 cups water
3 to 4 cups cubed (about 1 inch) Italian
    or sourdough bread, several days old
3 tablespoons lemon juice, or to taste
3 tablespoons honey or rice syrup, or
    to taste
½ cup dark or golden raisins, optional
Salt and freshly ground pepper to taste

Heat the oil in a large soup pot. Add the onion and garlic and sauté over medium heat until golden, about 10 minutes. Add the carrots, potatoes, cabbage, bell peppers, tomatoes, wine, paprika, cumin, and water. Bring to a simmer, then simmer gently, covered, for 30 to 40 minutes, or until the vegetables are tender.

In the meantime, preheat the oven to 300 degrees. Spread the bread cubes in a single layer and bake until golden and crisp, about 12 to 15 minutes. Remove from the oven and let stand until needed.

When the stew is done, stir in the lemon juice and honey or rice syrup. There should be a subtle sweet-sour flavor. If you'd like it to be more pronounced, add more lemon juice and/or honey or rice syrup to your liking. Stir in the raisins if desired and season to taste with salt and pepper. Simmer over very low heat for another 10 minutes. If time allows, let the stew stand off the heat for an hour or two before serving, then heat through as needed.

When ready to serve the stew, divide the bread cubes among the serving bowls and ladle the stew over them. The bread will absorb much of the liquid and add a tasty textural element to the stew.

| Calories: 240 | Total fat: 5 g | Protein: 4 g |
| Carbohydrate: 43 g | Cholesterol: 0 g | Sodium: 120 mg |

Spanish Garbanzo Stew

6 to 8 servings

This classic recipe is easy and quick to prepare using good quality canned chickpeas (as we more commonly refer to garbanzos. Serve with Tomato-Olive Bread (page 137) and a simple homemade coleslaw.

1½ tablespoons olive oil
1 large onion, chopped
3 to 4 cloves garlic, minced
1 large green bell pepper, cut into narrow
  1-inch-long strips
2 1-pound cans chickpeas, drained and rinsed
1 28-ounce can diced tomatoes, undrained
1 teaspoon ground cumin
1 teaspoon dried oregano
¼ teaspoon dried thyme
Dash of nutmeg
1 cup water
2 to 3 tablespoons chopped fresh parsley
Salt and lots of freshly ground pepper
  to taste
Hot cooked rice, optional

Heat the oil in a large soup pot. Add the onion and garlic and sauté over medium heat until the onion is translucent. Add the green pepper and continue to sauté until the onion is golden.

Add the chickpeas, tomatoes, cumin, oregano, thyme, and nutmeg, along with the water. Bring to a simmer, then cook at a steady simmer, covered, for 20 minutes.

Stir in the parsley and season sparingly with salt (the use of canned chickpeas might make salt completely unnecessary) and generously with pepper. Serve the stew in bowls on its own or over a small amount of hot cooked rice.

Calories: 210	Total fat: 5 g	Protein: 8 g
Carbohydrate: 33 g	Cholesterol: 0 g	Sodium: 18 mg

Chickpea and Bulgur Stew

6 to 8 servings

Bulgur (presteamed cracked wheat, commonly available in natural food stores) is not often used in soups, but works very nicely, adding protein and a chewy texture.

2½ tablespoons olive oil, divided
1 large onion, chopped
2 to 3 cloves garlic, minced
2 large celery stalks, diced
2 medium white turnips, peeled and diced
½ cup finely shredded cabbage
½ cup raw bulgur
1 28-ounce can diced tomatoes, undrained
2 bay leaves
2 teaspoons Italian herb mix
1 teaspoon paprika
4 cups water
1 1-pound can chickpeas, drained and rinsed
Salt and freshly ground pepper to taste
1 medium green bell pepper, cut into thin 1-inch-long strips

Heat 1½ tablespoons of the oil in a large soup pot. Add the onion and sauté over moderate heat until golden. Add all the remaining ingredients except for the last three, bring to a simmer, then simmer gently, covered, until the bulgur and all the vegetables are tender, about 35 to 40 minutes. Add the chickpeas, then season to taste with salt and pepper. Simmer for another 15 minutes. If time allows, let the soup stand for about an hour before serving, then heat through as needed.

Just before serving, heat the remaining tablespoon of olive oil in a small skillet. Sauté the bell pepper over medium-high heat until it is just lightly touched with brown spots. After ladling the soup into bowls, top each serving with some of the sautéed bell pepper.

Calories: 193	Total fat: 6 g	Protein: 6 g
Carbohydrate: 29 g	Cholesterol: 0 g	Sodium: 48 mg

Golden Curried Pea Soup

6 to 8 servings

The complementary protein of the peas and rice make this easy winter soup a natural choice as a hearty main dish. Make Whole Wheat Vegetable Muffins (page 139) to go along with it, plus a simple, palate-cooling salad of cucumbers dressed in yogurt.

2 tablespoons canola oil
1 cup finely chopped onion
8 cups water
1 large potato, peeled and diced
2 to 3 cloves garlic, crushed or minced
2 vegetable bouillon cubes
1 pound dried yellow split peas, rinsed
½ cup raw brown rice, rinsed
2 bay leaves
2 teaspoons good quality curry powder or
    garam masala, more or less to taste
1 teaspoon grated fresh ginger
Salt to taste

Heat the oil in a soup pot. Add the onion and sauté over moderately low heat until golden. Add all the remaining ingredients except the salt. Bring to a simmer, then simmer gently, covered, until the peas are mushy, about 1½ hours. Stir occasionally.

When the peas are done, adjust the consistency with more water as needed, then season to taste with salt. This soup thickens considerably as it stands; thin with additional water and adjust the seasonings.

Calories: 179	Total fat: 3 g	Protein: 6 g
Carbohydrate: 29 g	Cholesterol: 0 g	Sodium: 3 mg

To ensure a good crop, plant peas when the moon is waning, so that they may grow as it does, and thus bear plentifully.

— Old European folk belief

Curried Millet-Spinach Soup

8 servings

Millet, an exceptionally nutritious if rather bland grain, is used to great advantage in this soup, where it has an opportunity to soak up all the spicy flavors.

2 tablespoons canola oil or soy margarine
¾ cup raw millet, rinsed in a fine sieve
1 cup chopped onion
2 cloves garlic, minced
2 medium potatoes, scrubbed and diced
1 large carrot, peeled and coarsely
    chopped
1 14- to 16-ounce can diced tomatoes,
    undrained
1 teaspoon freshly grated ginger
2 teaspoons good quality curry powder or
    garam masala, more or less to taste
8 cups water
1 10-ounce package frozen chopped
    spinach, thawed
2 tablespoons finely chopped fresh parsley
Juice of ½ lemon
Salt and freshly ground pepper to taste
Plain low-fat yogurt for topping, optional

Combine all the ingredients except the last five in a large soup pot. Cover with the water. Bring to a simmer, then simmer gently, covered, for 1 to 1½ hours, or until the millet and vegetables are tender.

Stir in the spinach, parsley, and lemon juice. If the soup is too thick, add a bit more water. Season to taste with salt and pepper and simmer over very low heat for another 10 to 15 minutes.

This soup thickens as it stands, especially after refrigeration. Adjust the consistency with water, then correct the seasonings. Top each serving with a dollop of yogurt if desired.

| Calories: 196 | Total fat: 5 g | Protein: 5 g |
| Carbohydrate: 34 g | Cholesterol: 0 g | Sodium: 52 mg |

Spicy Chili Bean Soup

8 or more servings

For those who like "hot stuff," the hot chilies add a fiery kick to this soup. If you'd like a toned-down version, use mild chilies.

1 pound dried kidney, red, or pink beans
1 large onion, chopped
2 to 3 cloves garlic, minced
2 bay leaves
2 tablespoons olive oil, divided
1 14- to 16-ounce can diced tomatoes, undrained
¾ cup tomato sauce
⅓ cup raw brown rice, rinsed
2 teaspoons chili powder, more or less to taste
2 fresh hot green chilies, seeded and chopped
1 cup cooked fresh or thawed frozen corn kernels
Salt to taste
1 large green bell pepper, cut into l-inch strips
Grated reduced-fat cheddar cheese or cheddar-style soy cheese for topping, optional

Soak the beans overnight in plenty of water. Once you're ready to begin the soup, drain them and cover them with fresh water in a ratio of about double the water to the volume of beans. Add the onion and garlic, bring to a simmer, then simmer steadily, covered, for 1 to 1½ hours, or until the beans are tender (press one between your thumb and forefinger — if it yields easily, this is the right texture).

Add the bay leaves, half of the oil, the tomatoes, tomato sauce, rice, chili powder, and chopped chilies. Return to a simmer, then simmer gently over low heat until the rice is done, about 45 minutes or a bit longer. Stir in the corn kernels and season with salt. Continue to simmer over very low heat.

Heat the remaining olive oil in a small skillet. Add the green bell pepper and sauté over medium heat, stirring frequently, until it is fragrant and just lightly touched with brown. Remove from the heat.

Top each serving of soup with a few strips of sautéed bell pepper and a small quantity of grated cheese if desired.

| Calories: 179 | Total fat: 5 g | Protein: 6 g |
| Carbohydrate: 30 g | Cholesterol: 0 g | Sodium: 147 mg |

Brown Rice and Three-Bean Soup

8 servings

A warming, hearty, high-fiber soup, this is great served with Green Chili Cornbread (page 134) and a simple salad.

2 tablespoons olive oil
1 large onion, chopped
1 large celery stalk, diced
½ cup raw brown rice, rinsed
1 14- to 16-ounce can diced tomatoes, undrained
1½ teaspoons Italian herb mix
1 teaspoon chili powder
1 tablespoon soy sauce or tamari
6 cups water
½ pound green beans, trimmed and cut into ½- to 1-inch pieces, or 1 10-ounce package frozen green beans, unthawed
1 1-pound can Great Northern beans (cannellini), drained and rinsed
1 1-pound can kidney or red beans, drained and rinsed
1 tablespoon lemon juice
Salt and freshly ground pepper to taste

Heat the oil in a soup pot. Add the onion and sauté over medium heat until golden. Add the celery, rice, tomatoes, seasonings, and soy sauce or tamari, and water. Bring to a simmer, then simmer gently, covered, for 30 minutes. Add the three types of beans and simmer over very low heat for another 30 minutes or so, or until the rice and beans are quite tender. Stir in the lemon juice, then season to taste with salt and pepper. If time allows, let the soup stand for an hour or longer before serving, then heat through as needed.

Calories: 239   Total fat: 5 g   Protein: 11 g
Carbohydrate: 40 g   Cholesterol: 0 g   Sodium: 139 mg

Next to the Emperor, rice is the most sacred of all things on earth.

— Japanese proverb

Taco Soup

6 servings

The zesty flavors of tacos are turned inside out in this easy and offbeat soup. The presentation of this soup is fun and dramatic.

4 cups water, divided
½ cup raw bulgur (presteamed cracked wheat)
1 tablespoon canola oil
1 large onion, chopped
2 to 3 cloves garlic, minced
1 medium green bell pepper, finely diced
4 cups cooked or canned pinto beans (from 1½ cups raw beans or 2 1-pound cans, drained and rinsed)
1 28-ounce can crushed tomatoes
¼ cup chopped mild green chilies, fresh or canned, optional
¼ cup chopped fresh cilantro, optional
1 to 2 teaspoons chili powder, or to taste
1 teaspoon ground cumin

Garnishes:
Shredded romaine or green-leaf lettuce
Finely diced fresh plum tomatoes, about 4
Sliced black olives
Reduced-fat sour cream or plain low-fat yogurt
Large triangular low-fat tortilla chips

Bring 1 cup of the water to a boil in a small saucepan. Add the bulgur and simmer, covered, for 15 minutes, or until the water is absorbed. If making ahead of time, simply add the bulgur to the boiling water, cover, and remove from the heat. Let stand for 30 minutes.

Heat the oil in a soup pot. Add the onion and garlic and sauté over medium heat until translucent. Add the bell pepper and continue to sauté, stirring frequently, until the onion is golden.

Add the remaining ingredients, except the garnishes, plus the cooked bulgur and the remaining 3 cups of water. Stir together and bring to a simmer. Simmer steadily, covered, for 15 minutes, then remove from the heat.

Assemble each serving as follows: Fill each bowl about two thirds full with soup. Top with some shredded lettuce, diced tomatoes, and olive slices. Place a dollop of sour cream or yogurt in the center. Line the perimeter of each bowl with 5 or 6 tortilla chips, points facing upward. The effect will be star shaped. The tortilla chips can be used to scoop up the solid parts of the soup or just nibbled on with the soup. Pass around a bowl of extra tortilla chips.

Calories: 260	Total fat: 2 g	Protein: 11 g
Carbohydrate: 47 g	Cholesterol: 0 g	Sodium: 125 mg

Hearty Barley-Bean Soup

6 to 8 servings

This is a good, basic, everyday sort of soup, suitable for cold weather. Try Cheese and Herb Corn Muffins (page 140) with it.

2 tablespoons olive oil
2 large onions, chopped
2 cloves garlic, minced
¾ cup raw pearl or pot barley, rinsed
2 large celery stalks, diced
Handful of celery greens
1 bay leaf
2½ teaspoons salt-free herb-and-spice
 seasoning mix
1 14- to 16-ounce can diced tomatoes,
 undrained
6 cups water
1 1-pound can kidney, red, or pink beans,
 drained and rinsed
3 tablespoons chopped fresh parsley
2 tablespoons minced fresh dill
Salt and freshly ground pepper to taste

Heat the oil in a soup pot. Add the onions and garlic and sauté over moderate heat until the onions are golden. Add all the remaining ingredients except the last 4. Cover with the water. Bring to a simmer, then simmer gently, covered, for 1 hour. At this time the barley and vegetables should be tender. Add the beans, parsley, and dill. Season to taste with salt and pepper, then simmer for another 30 minutes over low heat.

Serve at once, or allow the soup to stand for an hour or so before serving, then heat through as needed. As the soup stands, it will thicken; adjust the consistency as needed with additional water, then correct the seasonings.

Calories: 193	Total fat: 5 g	Protein: 7 g
Carbohydrate: 32 g	Cholesterol: 0 g	Sodium: 20 mg

Barley...is more cooling than wheat, and a little cleansing; and all the preparations thereof do give great nourishment to persons troubled with fevers, agues, and heats in the stomach.

— Nicolas Culpeper
Culpeper's Complete Herbal, 1653

Creamy Mung Bean Soup

8 servings

Mung beans are small olive-colored legumes that are staples in Indian cookery. Look for them at natural food stores. Serve this soup with Barley or Rice Triangles (page 142), Oat-Chive Dumplings (page 152), or Chapatis (page 148).

1½ tablespoons canola oil
2 large onions, chopped
5 to 6 cloves garlic, minced
1 pound mung beans, rinsed
10 cups water
2 medium carrots, peeled and coarsely
　　chopped
1 teaspoon freshly grated ginger, more or
　　less to taste
1½ teaspoons good quality curry powder
　　or garam masala, more or less to taste
¼ cup chopped fresh cilantro or parsley
2 cups low-fat milk or soy milk, or as
　　needed
Salt and freshly ground pepper to taste

*Eat soup first and eat it last,
and live till a hundred years be
past.*

—French proverb

Heat the oil in a large soup pot. Add the onion and sauté over moderate heat until it is translucent. Add the garlic and continue to sauté until the onion is golden and just beginning to be touched with brown. Add the mung beans and water. Bring to a simmer, then cook at a steady but gentle simmer, covered, for 30 minutes. Add the carrots, ginger, and curry powder or garam masala. Simmer for another 1 to 1½ hours, or until the mung beans are tender and slightly mushy. Remove from the heat.

With a slotted spoon, transfer half of the solid ingredients to a food processor or blender, along with about ½ cup of the liquid. Process until smoothly pureed, then stir back into the soup pot. Stir in the cilantro or parsley, followed by enough milk or soy milk to give the soup a slightly thick consistency. Season to taste with salt and pepper. Simmer over very low heat for 15 minutes, then serve.

Calories: 130	Total fat: 4 g	Protein: 6 g
Carbohydrate: 19 g	Cholesterol: 3 g	Sodium: 42 mg

Tomato, Lentil, and Barley Soup

6 to 8 servings

Lentil soups are so satisfying in winter. Served with Quick Sunflower-Cheese Bread (page 134) or Focaccia Bread (page 138), this soup needs only a simple salad to make a very filling meal.

½ pound dry lentils, rinsed
¾ cup raw pearl or pot barley, rinsed
6 cups water
1 tablespoon olive oil
1 large onion, chopped
1 clove garlic, minced
2 large celery stalks, diced
2 medium carrots, peeled and sliced
1 cup shredded white cabbage
1 28-ounce can diced tomatoes, undrained
¼ cup dry red wine
1 tablespoon apple- cider vinegar
¼ cup chopped fresh parsley
2 teaspoons salt-free herb-and-spice seasoning mix
Salt and freshly ground pepper to taste

Combine the lentils and barley in a large soup pot with the water and bring to a simmer. Add all the remaining ingredients except the salt and pepper, return to a simmer, then simmer gently, covered, until everything is tender, about 45 to 55 minutes. Stir occasionally and add more water if the soup becomes too thick.

Season to taste with salt and pepper. If time allows, let the soup stand for an hour or so before serving, then heat through as needed.

Calories: 152	Total fat: 1 g	Protein: 5 g
Carbohydrate: 26 g	Cholesterol: 0 g	Sodium: 35 mg

The philosophers Virgil and Pliny credited lentils with the ability to produce temperaments of mildness and moderation in those who consumed them.

To improve the temperament of a surly husband, feed him lentils daily.

Curried Lentil, Potato, and Cauliflower Soup

6 to 8 servings

1½ tablespoons canola oil
1 large onion, chopped
6 cups water
1 cup lentils, rinsed
1 large celery stalk, diced
3 to 4 cloves garlic, minced
2 bay leaves
2 large potatoes, scrubbed and diced
1 14- to 16-ounce can diced tomatoes,
    undrained
2 teaspoons good quality curry powder or
    garam masala, more or less to taste
2½ cups finely chopped cauliflower
    pieces
1 cup finely chopped fresh spinach leaves
2 tablespoons chopped fresh cilantro
Juice of ½ lemon
Salt and freshly ground pepper to taste

Heat the oil in a soup pot. Add the onion and sauté over moderately low heat until it is golden. Add the water, lentils, celery, garlic, and bay leaves. Bring to a simmer, then simmer gently, covered, for about 10 minutes.

Add the potatoes, tomatoes, and curry powder or garam masala, and simmer until the potatoes are about half done, about 10 to 15 minutes. Add the cauliflower and simmer until the lentils and vegetables are tender, another 20 minutes or so. Stir in the spinach, cilantro, and lemon juice. Adjust the consistency with more water if necessary, then season to taste with salt and pepper. Simmer over very low heat for another 5 minutes. Serve at once, or let stand for an hour before serving, then heat through as needed.

Calories: 152	Total fat: 2 g	Protein: 6 g
Carbohydrate: 26 g	Cholesterol: 0 g	Sodium: 54 mg

Four-Grain Tomato Soup

8 or more servings

A savory medley of whole grains and vegetables in a tomato base. For a hearty combination, serve with Savory Bean Bread (page 136) or, for a lighter accompaniment, with Bruschetta (page 150) or Parmesan Pita Wedges (page 148).

1 tablespoon canola oil

2 medium onions, quartered and thinly sliced

2 large celery stalks, finely diced

2 medium carrots, peeled and finely diced

2 medium potatoes, scrubbed and diced, or 2 large turnips, peeled and diced

1 28-ounce can pureed or crushed tomatoes

¼ cup brown rice, any variety (see note)

¼ cup wild rice

¼ cup millet

¼ cup medium pearl barley

2 bay leaves

2 teaspoons salt-free herb-and-spice seasoning mix

6 cups water

¼ cup chopped fresh dill (if unavailable, use 2 teaspoons dried dill)

Salt and freshly ground pepper to taste

Heat the oil in a soup pot. Add the onion and sauté over medium heat for 5 to 8 minutes, until translucent. Add the celery, carrots, potatoes or turnips, tomatoes, the four grains, bay leaves, and seasoning mix. If not using fresh dill, add the dried dill now as well. Stir in the water and bring to a simmer. Simmer gently, covered, for 1 hour, stirring every 15 minutes or so.

If the soup is too dense, adjust with additional water and return to a gentle simmer. Add the fresh dill and season to taste with salt and pepper. Simmer gently for another 15 to 20 minutes, or until the grains and vegetables are tender. Serve at once, or let the soup stand off the heat for an hour or two before serving, then heat through as needed.

This soup thickens quite a bit as it stands. Add water as needed and adjust the seasonings.

Note: If you use brown basmati rice, the soup will give off a marvelous scent as it cooks.

Calories: 138	Total fat: 2 g	Protein: 3 g
Carbohydrate: 26 g	Cholesterol: 0 g	Sodium: 50 mg

Vegetarian Goulash

8 servings

A satisfying meatless take on the classic Hungarian goulash, this makes good use of seitan, a high-protein, low-fat meat substitute. Seitan is available from natural food stores in ready-to-use form. You might also explore the use of Arrowhead Mills's Seitan Quick Mix, which is more economical and allows you to make seitan easily whenever you'd like. For a complete and hearty meal, serve with hot buttered noodles sprinkled with poppy seeds, plus a green salad.

2½ tablespoons canola oil, divided
1½ cups chopped onions
2 cloves garlic, minced
2 tablespoons unbleached white flour
4 medium potatoes, scrubbed and cut into
    ¾-inch chunks
3 medium carrots, peeled and sliced
1 14- to 16-ounce can diced tomatoes,
    undrained
¼ cup dry red wine, optional
1 tablespoon paprika
4 cups cooking liquid from seitan,
    Light Vegetable Stock (page 7), or
    water
2 cups frozen green beans, thawed
2 tablespoons minced fresh parsley
Salt to taste
1 tablespoon soy sauce or tamari
2 pounds seitan, cut into approximately
    1-inch chunks

Heat half of the oil in a soup pot. Add the onion and sauté over medium heat until translucent. Add the garlic and continue to sauté until the onion is golden. Sprinkle in the flour, stirring in until it is well blended with the onions. Add the potatoes, carrots, tomatoes, optional wine, and paprika, and cover with the liquid, stock, or water. Bring to a simmer, then simmer gently, covered, for 45 minutes.

Add the green beans and parsley, then season to taste with salt. Simmer gently for another 15 minutes.

In the meantime, slowly heat the remaining oil and soy sauce or tamari together in a skillet over medium heat. Add the seitan chunks and stir quickly to coat with the oil and soy sauce or tamari mixture. Raise the heat to medium-high and sauté, stirring frequently, until the chunks are somewhat crispy and golden on most sides, about 10 minutes. Remove from the heat and stir into the stew. Serve at once, or let stand for several hours before serving and heat through as needed.

Calories: 346	Total fat: 5 g	Protein: 41 g
Carbohydrate: 33 g	Cholesterol: 0 g	Sodium: 175 mg

Mock Chicken-Noodle Soup

6 servings

This simple, delicious soup recalls a comfort soup from my childhood. It proves that winter soups need not always be thick and hearty to provide a sense of warmth. Baked pressed tofu, a chewy, seasoned product, makes a marvelous stand-in for chicken. It is widely available in natural food stores, sold in cellophane packages.

1 tablespoon canola oil
8 cups plus 2 tablespoons water
2 large celery stalks, finely diced
3 medium carrots, peeled and thinly
    sliced
2 to 3 cloves garlic, minced
1 small onion, minced
2 vegetable bouillon cubes
1 teaspoon salt-free herb-and-spice
    seasoning mix
½ teaspoon dried dill
6 ounces short, fine egg noodles,
    preferably yolk free
6 ounces baked pressed tofu, finely diced
Salt and freshly ground pepper to taste

Heat the oil slowly with 2 tablespoons of water in a large soup pot. Add the celery, carrots, garlic, and onion. Sauté over medium heat for 10 minutes, or until the vegetables begin to soften. Add 8 cups of water, the bouillon cubes, seasoning mix, and dried dill. Bring to a simmer, then cook at a gentle simmer for 15 minutes, or until the vegetables are tender.

Raise the heat and bring to a more vigorous simmer. Add the noodles and cook at a steady simmer for 5 to 8 minutes, or until the noodles are al dente. Add the diced tofu, then season to taste with salt and pepper. Serve at once.

Note: As the soup stands, the noodles quickly absorb the liquid. If you plan on having leftovers of the soup, add a cup or so of additional water before storing and adjust the seasonings. That way the soup can develop more flavor as it stands.

Calories: 101	Total fat: 4 g	Protein: 4 g
Carbohydrate: 12 g	Cholesterol: 9 g	Sodium: 33 mg

Mixed Mushroom Soup with Bok Choy

4 to 6 servings

An elegant and aromatic brothy soup, this lifts the senses on a cold winter day, though it can be enjoyed at other times of the year. This is an excellent way to whet the appetite for an Oriental-style vegetable stir-fry.

1 recipe Oriental Mushroom Broth (page 11), shiitake mushrooms reserved
1½ cups sliced small white mushrooms
2 fresh portabello mushrooms, about 4 inches in diameter, thinly sliced, then cut into bite-sized pieces
¼ cup dry white wine
5 to 6 stalks bok choy, greens included, thinly sliced
3 to 4 scallions, white and green parts, sliced
2 to 3 tablespoons soy sauce or tamari, or to taste
Lemon-pepper to taste

Bring the broth to a simmer. Trim the stems off of the shiitakes used to make the broth, then slice the caps and return them to the broth along with the white and portabello mushrooms and wine. Simmer gently for 10 to 15 minutes, covered, or until the fresh mushrooms are done but still pleasantly chewy.

Add the remaining ingredients and simmer for another 5 to 8 minutes, just until the bok choy is crisp-tender. Serve at once.

| Calories: 74 | Total fat: 2 g | Protein: 3 g |
| Carbohydrate: 9 g | Cholesterol: 0 g | Sodium: 506 mg |

I am a mushroom
On whom the dew of heaven
Drops now and then.

—John Ford (1586–1639)
The Broken Heart

Miso Soup with Winter Vegetables

6 servings

This winter miso soup is very warming. See page 9, under Simple Miso Broth, for further information on miso.

1 tablespoon canola or peanut oil

2 medium onions, quartered and sliced

4 medium potatoes, peeled and finely diced

1½ cups shredded savoy or white cabbage

1 large celery stalk, cut in matchstick-shaped pieces

1 large carrot, peeled and cut in matchstick-shaped pieces

1 recipe Oriental Mushroom Broth (page 11), shiitake mushrooms reserved

¼ cup dry red wine or sherry

1 teaspoon freshly grated ginger

½ teaspoon lemon-pepper

2 to 3 tablespoons miso, to taste

Heat the oil in a soup pot. Add the onions and sauté over medium heat until golden. Add the potatoes, cabbage, celery, carrot, and the Oriental Mushroom Broth. Trim the shiitake mushrooms used in making the broth of their tough stems, then slice the caps and add them to the soup along with the red wine or sherry, ginger, and lemon-pepper. Bring to a simmer, then simmer gently, covered, for 25 to 30 minutes, or until the vegetables are done but still have a bit of firmness.

Dissolve the miso in just enough water to make it smooth and pourable. Stir it into the soup, then remove the soup from the heat and serve at once.

Calories: 200	Total fat: 4 g	Protein: 3 g
Carbohydrate: 30 g	Cholesterol: 0 g	Sodium: 274 mg

S · P · R · I · N · G

After the thick, hearty soups of winter, those presented here offer the palate a lift with lighter textures and flavors. These soups set the stage for a meal, taking the edge off of hunger yet leaving room for other courses.

Spring Vegetable Soup

8 to 10 servings

Brimming with fresh produce in a light, mildly seasoned broth, this is just the soup to serve as an introduction to a festive spring meal such as an Easter dinner or a Passover seder. If you do use it for Passover, whip up some matzo balls from a matzo meal mix, which provides a foolproof recipe right on the package.

2 tablespoons olive oil

1 medium onion, finely chopped

2 large or 3 medium leeks, white parts only, quartered lengthwise, chopped, and well rinsed

2 medium potatoes, peeled and diced

2 medium white turnips, peeled and diced

3 medium carrots, peeled and sliced

3 medium celery stalks, diced

½ pound small white mushrooms, sliced

8 cups Light Vegetable Stock (page 7; increase the recipe by half), or 8 cups water with 2 vegetable bouillon cubes

1 teaspoon paprika

1 teaspoon ground cumin

2 cups frozen green peas, thawed

Salt and freshly ground pepper to taste

Heat the oil in a soup pot. Add the onion and leeks and sauté over moderate heat until the leeks are limp, about 10 minutes. Add the potatoes, turnips, carrots, celery, mushrooms, stock or water, paprika, and cumin. Bring to a simmer, then simmer gently, covered, until the vegetables are tender, about 45 minutes.

Add the peas, then season to taste with salt and pepper. Let stand for several hours or overnight to develop flavor. Reheat when needed.

Calories: 165	Total fat: 2 g	Protein: 4 g
Carbohydrate: 29 g	Cholesterol: 0 g	Sodium: 71 mg

Greek-Flavored Spinach and Orzo Soup

6 to 8 servings

A lively, lemony soup that comes together quickly. Serve with fresh store-bought pita.

1½ tablespoons olive oil
1 cup chopped onion or sliced leek
1 large red bell pepper, diced
2 to 3 cloves garlic, minced
¾ cup orzo (rice-shaped pasta)
5 cups Light Vegetable Stock (page 7)
     or 5 cups water with 1 vegetable
     bouillon cube
1 14-ounce can diced tomatoes,
     undrained
5 to 6 ounces fresh spinach, washed,
     stemmed, and chopped
¼ cup chopped fresh parsley or dill,
     or a combination, or more to taste
Juice of 1 lemon
Lemon-pepper to taste
Salt to taste

Heat the oil in a soup pot. Add the onion or leek and sauté over medium heat until translucent, about 5 minutes. Add the red pepper and garlic and sauté the vegetables for another 5 to 8 minutes, or until the onion or leek turns golden and the red pepper softens.

In the meantime, cook the orzo in a separate saucepan until al dente. When done, drain.

Add the stock or water and the tomatoes to the soup pot. Bring to a simmer, then simmer steadily, covered, for 10 minutes.

Add the cooked orzo to the soup along with the spinach and herbs. Stir in the lemon juice, then season to taste with lemon-pepper and salt. Serve at once.

Calories: 134	Total fat: 2 g	Protein: 4 g
Carbohydrate: 22 g	Cholesterol: 0 g	Sodium: 45 mg

When buying spinach, assess its liveliness. It should have a bouncing, bright appearance. As you stuff it into your basket...it should crunch and squeak.

— Jane Grigson
Jane Grigson's Vegetable Book, 1978

Asparagus and Spinach Soup
with Wild Rice and Wild Mushrooms

6 servings

An earthy, elegant medley of colors, textures, and flavors.

2 cups water
½ cup uncooked wild rice, rinsed
10 to 12 ounces asparagus
4 to 6 ounces fresh wild mushrooms, such
   as porcini or shiitake
1 large carrot, peeled and coarsely grated
1 medium yellow summer squash, diced
4 to 5 scallions, white and green parts, sliced
1 recipe Onion or Leek and Garlic Broth
   (page 8), Oriental Mushroom Broth
   (page 11), or 6 cups water with 2
   vegetable bouillon cubes
1½ teaspoons salt-free herb-and-spice
   seasoning mix
¼ cup dry white wine, optional
5 to 6 ounces fresh spinach, washed,
   stemmed, and chopped
Salt and freshly ground pepper to taste

Bring the water to a boil in a small saucepan. Add the wild rice, then cook at a gentle simmer, covered, until the water is absorbed, about 35 minutes.

Meanwhile, trim the asparagus of its woody ends and scrape the bottom third of the stalk if the skin looks tough. Cut into 1-inch pieces.

Combine the asparagus with the remaining ingredients, except the last 2, in a soup pot and bring to a simmer. There should be enough liquid to just cover the vegetables; adjust if necessary. Simmer gently, covered, for about 15 minutes, or until the vegetables are just tender. Remove from the heat.

When the wild rice is done, stir it into the soup along with the spinach. Season to taste with salt and pepper. Let the soup stand for an hour or two before serving, then heat through as needed.

Calories: 123	Total fat: 2 g	Protein: 3 g
Carbohydrate: 17 g	Cholesterol: 0 g	Sodium: 101 mg

Asparagus is a delicate fruit, and wholesome for everiebodie, and especially when it is thicke, tender and sweet...it maketh a good color in the face.

— Anonymous
Maison Rustique, 1600

Puree of Asparagus with Buckwheat Noodles

6 servings

Nutty-tasting dark buckwheat noodles, traditional to Japan, add an unusual element to this soup. Look for them in natural food stores or Oriental groceries.

2 pounds asparagus
1 tablespoon dark sesame oil
1 large onion, chopped
2 large celery stalks, diced
2 medium potatoes, scrubbed and diced
4½ cups Light Vegetable Stock
    (page 7) or water with 1 vegetable
    bouillon cube
1½ teaspoons salt-free herb-and-spice
    seasoning mix
2 tablespoons soy sauce or tamari
4 ounces buckwheat noodles (soba)
Freshly ground pepper to taste
Slivered or chopped almonds for garnish
Minced chives or scallions for garnish

Trim the woody ends from the asparagus, peel any tough skin with a vegetable peeler, and cut into 1-inch lengths. Reserve and set aside the tips.

Heat the oil in a large soup pot. Add the onion and sauté over medium heat until golden. Add the celery, potatoes, stock or water, seasoning mix, and soy sauce or tamari. Bring to a simmer, then simmer gently, covered, for 10 minutes. Add the asparagus pieces (not the tips) and simmer for another 15 minutes, or until the vegetables are tender. Remove from the heat.

With a slotted spoon transfer the solid ingredients to a food processor or blender. Puree in batches until smooth and stir back into the liquid in the soup pot. Return to very low heat. Correct the consistency if necessary with additional water or stock, then taste to correct the seasonings.

Break the buckwheat noodles into 1-to-2-inch lengths. In a separate saucepan, cook them in rapidly simmering water until they are al dente. Drain and rinse them briefly under cool water. At the same time, steam the reserved asparagus tips until they are bright green. Stir both the noodles and asparagus tips into the soup. Add freshly ground pepper to taste and remove from the heat.

Serve at once, garnishing each serving with the almonds and chives or scallions.

Calories: 158	Total fat: 3 g	Protein: 5 g
Carbohydrate: 27 g	Cholesterol: 0 g	Sodium: 378 mg

Spicy Asparagus and Green Bean Stew

6 servings

I enjoy the tender green beans of spring, though I do find them to be a temperamental vegetable. That's why I recommend steaming the green beans separately, and adding them once the asparagus is crisp-tender.

1 pound fresh green beans, trimmed and cut in half

1 tablespoon dark sesame oil

1 medium onion, finely chopped

4 to 5 cloves garlic, minced

1 pound slender asparagus, woody ends trimmed, cut into 1½-inch lengths

2 medium red bell peppers, cut into narrow strips approximately 1½ inches in length

2 to 3 teaspoons grated fresh ginger, to taste

¼ cup dry red wine

2 cups water

1 8-ounce package baked tofu (available at natural food stores), diced

1 teaspoon hot chili oil or chili powder, or more to taste

1 tablespoon rice vinegar or white wine vinegar

2 to 3 tablespoons soy sauce or tamari, or to taste

2 tablespoons cornstarch

Hot cooked rice or noodles, optional

In a large saucepan, steam the green beans in an inch or two of water, covered, until crisp-tender. Stir occasionally. When done, remove from the heat and rinse briefly with cool water to stop the cooking process.

In the meantime, heat the oil in a soup pot or large steep-sided wok. Add the onion and garlic and sauté over medium heat, stirring frequently, until the onion is lightly golden. Add the asparagus, red pepper strips, ginger, wine, and water. Bring to a simmer, then simmer gently, covered, for 10 minutes, or until the asparagus and red pepper strips are crisp-tender.

Add the tofu, chili oil or chili powder, vinegar, and soy sauce or tamari. Once the green beans are done, add them as well. Stir gently and bring the mixture to a simmer.

Dissolve the cornstarch in a small amount of water. Pour slowly into the stew, stirring. Simmer over low heat, uncovered, for another 10 minutes. Serve at once over hot cooked rice or noodles or on its own.

Calories: 129   Total fat: 4 g   Protein: 6 g
Carbohydrate: 15 g   Cholesterol: 0 g   Sodium: 431 mg

Creole Lima Bean Stew

6 to 8 servings

Just the thing to serve on a chilly, rainy early spring day. Green Chili Cornbread (page 135) or fresh store-bought cornbread marries well with these flavors.

1 tablespoon canola oil
1 large onion, quartered and thinly sliced
3 celery stalks, thinly sliced
1 large green or red bell pepper, diced
2 tablespoons unbleached white flour
2 cups water
4 cups (2 10-ounce packages) frozen baby lima beans, thawed
1 1-pound can red kidney beans, drained and rinsed
1 28-ounce can diced tomatoes, undrained
1 teaspoon salt-free herb-and-spice seasoning mix
2 bay leaves
½ teaspoon each dried basil and dried thyme
¼ teaspoon dried red pepper flakes or pinch of cayenne pepper, or more or less to taste
Salt and freshly ground pepper to taste
¼ to ½ cup chopped fresh parsley
Hot cooked rice, optional

Heat the oil in a large soup pot. Add the onion and sauté over medium heat until translucent. Add the celery and bell pepper and sauté for another 5 minutes. Slowly sprinkle in and stir in the flour, then add the water and all the remaining ingredients except the salt, pepper, and parsley. Bring to a simmer, then simmer gently, covered, for 40 to 45 minutes.

Season to taste with salt and pepper, then stir in the fresh parsley. The stew should be thick, but add a small amount of water if it seems too dense. Adjust the other seasonings if needed.

Serve in bowls on its own or over hot cooked rice, if desired.

Calories: 228	Total fat: 2 g	Protein: 12 g
Carbohydrate: 40 g	Cholesterol: 0 g	Sodium: 57 mg

Leek and Mushroom Bisque

6 to 8 servings

Farina (Cream of Wheat) is the secret to the smooth, thick texture of this soup.

3 large leeks
2 tablespoons soy margarine or canola oil
5 cups water
1 14-ounce can pureed tomatoes
½ cup farina (Cream of Wheat)
12 ounces mushrooms, coarsely chopped
    or sliced
2 teaspoons salt-free herb-and-spice
    seasoning mix
1½ to 2 cups low-fat milk or soy milk,
    or as needed
Salt and freshly ground pepper to taste

Slice the white part of the leeks into ¼-inch slices. Separate the slices into rings, then rinse well to remove all grit. Wash the green parts of the leeks well and cut them into halves.

Heat the margarine or oil in a soup pot. Add the white parts of the leeks and sauté over moderate heat until they are limp. Add the water and then the tomato puree. Bring to a simmer, then lower the heat until the liquid is at a very gentle simmer. Slowly sprinkle in the farina, stirring it in as you do. Add the green parts of the leeks, the mushrooms, and the seasoning mix. Cover and simmer gently for 35 minutes. Remove the green parts of the leeks and discard.

Stir in enough milk or soy milk to give a slightly thick consistency, then season to taste with salt and pepper. Simmer for another 5 minutes. Remove from the heat and let the soup stand for at least an hour before serving. Heat through as needed, then adjust the consistency with more milk or soy milk if necessary, and correct the seasonings. Serve at once.

Calories: 136   Total fat: 3 g   Protein: 4 g
Carbohydrate: 20 g   Cholesterol: 3 g   Sodium: 105 mg

"Cream" of Cauliflower Soup

6 servings

This dairy-free "cream" soup, enhanced with any of the garnishes recommended, is a simple, fresh introduction for a spring meal. With the very mild flavor of cauliflower as its base, this soup benefits from a well-flavored stock to heighten its flavor.

1 tablespoon canola oil or soy margarine

1 cup chopped onion

2 to 4 cloves garlic, minced

1 large head cauliflower, chopped into 2-inch chunks

2 medium potatoes, peeled and diced

6 cups Onion or Leek and Garlic Broth (page 8) or water with 2 vegetable bouillon cubes

2 teaspoons salt-free herb-and-spice seasoning mix

1 teaspoon ground coriander

1 cup canned Great Northern beans (cannellini), drained and rinsed

Salt and freshly ground pepper to taste

Garnishes (choose any 2 or 3 of the following):

Steamed, finely chopped broccoli florets (about 1 cup)

Steamed chopped escarole or kale (about 1 cup)

Steamed fresh green peas (about ¾ cup)

Steamed red bell pepper strips (from about 1 large pepper)

Chopped fresh herbs (about ½ cup), such as a combination of parsley, dill, chives, and oregano

Heat the oil or margarine in a soup pot and add the onion and garlic. Sauté over medium heat until the onion is golden, about 10 minutes. Add the cauliflower, potatoes, broth or water, and seasonings. There should be enough broth or water to cover all but about an inch of the vegetables. Bring to a simmer, then simmer gently, covered, until the vegetables are tender, about 25 minutes. Remove from the heat.

Transfer the vegetables from the soup pot to a food processor or blender and puree in batches until smooth. Puree about half of the beans with each of two batches of vegetables. Transfer the puree back into the soup pot, stirring it back into whatever liquid remained. Let the soup stand for 1 to 2 hours before serving, then heat through as needed. Ladle into soup bowls and garnish the tops with 2 or 3 of the garnishes.

Calories: 171	Total fat: 4 g	Protein: 4 g
Carbohydrate: 26 g	Cholesterol: 0 g	Sodium: 28 mg

Curried Cauliflower-Cheese Soup

6 to 8 servings

1 tablespoon canola oil

2 tablespoons water

1 large onion, chopped

2 medium celery stalks, diced

3 medium potatoes, peeled and cut into
½-inch dice

1 medium head cauliflower, finely chopped

Light Vegetable Stock (page 7) or water,
as needed

2 teaspoons good quality curry powder or
garam masala, more or less to taste

1 cup low-fat milk or soy milk, or as needed

1 cup steamed fresh green peas or thawed
frozen green peas

3 tablespoons minced fresh dill or 1 tablespoon dried dill

1 cup firmly packed grated mild white
cheese, such as Monterey Jack or
mozzarella-style soy cheese

Salt and freshly ground pepper to taste

Heat the oil and water slowly in a soup pot. Add the onion and celery and sauté over moderately low heat until the onion is golden. Add the potatoes, cauliflower, and enough stock or water to barely cover. Stir in the curry powder or garam masala. Bring to a simmer, then simmer gently, covered, until all the vegetables are tender, about 20 to 25 minutes. Remove from the heat.

With a slotted spoon, transfer half of the solid ingredients to a food processor or blender. Process until smoothly pureed. Stir back into the remaining soup. Add just enough milk or soy milk to achieve a slightly thick consistency. Stir in the peas and dill, then return to low heat and bring to a gentle simmer. Sprinkle the cheese in a bit at a time, stirring in until fairly well melted each time (soy cheese may not melt as completely).

Adjust the consistency with more milk or soy milk if necessary, then season to taste with salt and pepper. Serve once the soup is heated through.

Calories: 219	Total fat: 7 g	Protein: 9 g
Carbohydrate: 29 g	Cholesterol: 16 g	Sodium: 147 mg

Curried Cashew Soup

6 to 8 servings

Cashews make an unusual and rich-tasting base for a soup. This delicious soup is good hot or at room temperature.

1½ tablespoons canola oil

2 large onions, chopped

3 to 4 cloves garlic, minced

1 large celery stalk, diced

1 cup toasted cashew pieces

1 teaspoon minced fresh ginger

5 cups water, divided

2 teaspoons good quality curry powder or garam masala, more or less to taste

1 tablespoon lemon juice

Juice of 1 fresh orange

3 cups steamed fresh green vegetables (such as finely chopped broccoli, green peas, diced zucchini, or any combination)

Salt to taste

Finely sliced scallions for garnish

Chopped cashews for garnish, optional

Heat the oil in a skillet. Add the onion, garlic, and celery and sauté over medium heat until all are lightly browned. Remove from the heat.

Place the cashews in a food processor and process until finely ground. Add the onion mixture from the skillet, the ginger, and 1 cup of the water. Process until well pureed.

Transfer the mixture into a large soup pot along with the rest of the water, the curry powder or garam masala, and lemon and orange juices. Bring to a simmer, then simmer gently over low heat for 30 minutes. Remove from the heat and let stand for 30 minutes to 1 hour.

Return to medium heat. Add the steamed vegetables and adjust if necessary with more water to achieve a slightly thick consistency. Season to taste with salt, then serve once the soup is heated through. Garnish each serving with a sprinkling of scallion and, if desired, a few chopped cashews.

Calories: 179	Total fat: 12 g	Protein: 4 g
Carbohydrate: 13 g	Cholesterol: 0 g	Sodium: 20 mg

Curried Vegetable Stew

6 to 8 servings

Spicy and savory, this hearty curry becomes the centerpiece of a satisfying meal served over hot cooked grains and accompanied by Chapatis (page 148) and a simple, palate-cooling salad of sliced cucumbers in yogurt. *↳Pita Wedges*

2 tablespoons canola oil
1 medium onion, chopped
2 to 3 cloves garlic, minced
2 cups baby carrots

Pre-cook → 1 medium eggplant, peeled and diced
2 medium potatoes, scrubbed and diced
1 large green or red bell pepper, diced
1 14-ounce can stewed or diced tomatoes, undrained
1 teaspoon grated fresh ginger
1 to 2 fresh chilies, seeded and minced, or canned chopped green chilies, to taste
1 to 2 teaspoons good quality curry powder or garam masala, to taste
1½ cups water
1 cup frozen green peas, thawed
¼ cup chopped fresh cilantro, optional
Salt to taste
Hot cooked grains (basmati rice, barley, or couscous), optional
Plain low-fat yogurt or soy yogurt for topping, optional

Heat the oil in a soup pot and add the onion, garlic, and baby carrots. Sauté over medium heat until the onion is golden, stirring frequently, about 10 minutes.

Add the eggplant, potatoes, bell pepper, tomatoes, ginger, chilies, and curry powder or garam masala, and water. Bring to a simmer, then cook, covered, at a gentle simmer until the vegetables are tender but not overdone.

Stir in the peas and cilantro and season to taste with salt. Taste for spiciness and adjust the seasonings as desired. Mash some of the potato dice with a wooden spoon to thicken the cooking liquid. Simmer over low heat, uncovered, for an additional 5 to 10 minutes. The vegetables should be enveloped in a thick liquid.

Serve in bowls alone or over hot cooked grains. If desired, top each serving with a dollop of yogurt or soy yogurt.

Variation: You may substitute other vegetables for the ones listed above. Instead of eggplant, try substituting a medium head of cauliflower, chopped into bite-sized pieces, or use corn kernels in place of the peas. Sweet potato may be used in place of white potato.

Calories: 156	Total fat: 3 g	Protein: 3 g
Carbohydrate: 26 g	Cholesterol: 0 g	Sodium: 43 mg

Country Captain Stew

6 servings

Though undoubtedly Indian influenced (it bears a passing resemblance to the classic East Indian mulligatawny soup), this is actually an adaptation of a classic curried chicken stew recipe from the American South. This meatless version substitutes chunks of tofu, baked until chewy and golden, for chicken. The harmony of sweet and savory flavors in a curried base is most appealing.

1 pound firm tofu
1 tablespoon canola oil
1½ cups chopped onion
3 to 4 cloves garlic, minced
1 large green bell pepper, cut into strips
4 medium potatoes, scrubbed and cut
    into ½-inch dice
1 14-ounce can diced tomatoes, undrained
2 Granny Smith apples, peeled, cored,
    and diced
1 to 2 teaspoons good quality curry
    powder or garam masala, to taste
1 teaspoon grated fresh ginger
2 cups water
½ cup dark raisins
⅓ cup chopped fresh cilantro or parsley
Salt to taste
Plain low-fat yogurt for topping, optional

Preheat the oven to 350 degrees.

Cut the tofu into ½-inch-thick slices and blot between clean tea towels or paper towels. Then cut into approximately ½-inch dice. Lightly oil a nonstick baking sheet and arrange the tofu dice on it in a single layer. Bake for 15 minutes, then carefully stir. Bake for another 10 to 15 minutes, stirring every 5 minutes, or until the tofu pieces are golden on most sides.

In the meantime, heat the oil in a soup pot. Add the onion and garlic and sauté over medium heat, stirring occasionally, until the onion is golden, about 10 to 12 minutes. Add the bell pepper, potatoes, tomatoes, apples, curry powder or garam masala, and ginger, along with the water. Bring to a simmer, then simmer gently, covered, for about 20 minutes, or until the potatoes are done.

Stir in the baked tofu, raisins, and cilantro or parsley. Season to taste with salt. Cook over low heat for another 10 to 15 minutes. Serve at once, or make ahead and reheat when needed. Top each serving with a scoop of yogurt if desired.

Calories: 246   Total fat: 6 g   Protein: 8 g
Carbohydrate: 41 g   Cholesterol: 0 g   Sodium: 21 mg

Creole Eggplant Soup

6 servings

Courtesy of the famous Commander's Palace restaurant in New Orleans, this soup was a favorite discovery while I was on a journey across the American South.

2 tablespoons canola oil
1 large onion, chopped
3 medium celery stalks, diced
1 clove garlic, minced
1½ tablespoons unbleached white flour
2 large potatoes, peeled and finely diced
1 large or 2 medium eggplants (1½ pounds total), peeled and finely diced
1 teaspoon dried basil
¼ teaspoon dried thyme
1 teaspoon good quality curry powder or garam masala
2 to 3 tablespoons chopped fresh parsley
1 cup low-fat milk or soy milk, or as needed
Salt and freshly ground pepper to taste

Heat the oil in a large soup pot. Add the onion, celery, and garlic and sauté over low heat, stirring frequently, for 10 minutes. Add a small amount of water if the mixture becomes dry. Sprinkle in the flour and cook, stirring, for another minute.

Place the potato and eggplant dice in the soup pot along with enough water to cover all but about an inch of the vegetables. Bring to a simmer. At this point you should be able to push all the vegetables below the water. Add the seasonings and stir well. Cover and simmer gently for 40 minutes, or until the vegetables are quite tender.

Stir in the parsley and enough milk or soy milk to achieve a slightly thick consistency. Season to taste with salt and pepper. Simmer over very low heat for another 5 to 10 minutes and serve, or let the soup stand off the heat for an hour or so, then heat through as needed.

Calories: 151   Total fat: 5 g   Protein: 3 g
Carbohydrate: 23 g   Cholesterol: 2 g   Sodium: 47 mg

Mediterranean Eggplant Soup

6 to 8 servings

A colorful medley of Italian flavors, this soup is a perfect introduction to a light meal — perhaps an omelet, a salad of crisp greens, and a good white wine. Serve with Parmesan Pita Wedges (page 148) or Bruschetta (page 150).

2 tablespoons olive oil
1 large onion, chopped
2 cloves garlic, pressed or minced
2 large celery stalks, finely diced
5 cups water
2 medium eggplants (about 1 ½ pounds in all), peeled and cut into ½-inch dice
1 28-ounce can diced tomatoes, undrained
2 teaspoons Italian herb mix
1 cup raw pasta, any small shape such as shells or twists
¼ cup finely chopped fresh parsley
Salt and freshly ground pepper to taste

Heat the oil in a soup pot. Add the onion, garlic, and celery and sauté over medium heat until the onion is golden. Add the water, eggplant dice, tomatoes, and herb mix. Bring to a simmer, then simmer gently, covered, until the eggplant is tender, about 45 minutes.

In the meantime, cook the pasta separately until it is al dente. Drain and stir into the soup along with the parsley. Adjust the consistency with more water if the soup has gotten too thick. Season to taste with salt and pepper. Simmer over very low heat another 15 minutes. Serve at once, or let the soup stand for an hour or so before serving, then heat through as needed.

Calories: 146	Total fat: 4 g	Protein: 4 g
Carbohydrate: 24 g	Cholesterol: 0 g	Sodium: 26 mg

White Bean Puree with Zucchini and Herbs

6 to 8 servings

Any of the dumplings on pages 151 to 153 add a nice touch to this soup, or serve it with any of the muffins on pages 139 to 141.

2 tablespoons canola oil, divided

1 large onion, chopped

1 clove garlic, minced

4 cups well-cooked or canned Great Northern beans (from about 1⅔ cups raw or 2 1-pound cans, drained and rinsed), divided

4 cups cooking liquid from beans, Light Vegetable Stock (page 7), or water with 1 vegetable bouillon cube

¼ cup dry white wine

3 tablespoons each chopped fresh parsley and minced fresh dill

1 teaspoon good quality curry powder or garam masala

1 medium zucchini

1 tablespoon water

Juice of ½ to 1 lemon, to taste

Salt and freshly ground pepper to taste

Heat half of the oil in a skillet. Add the onion and sauté over moderate heat until it is translucent. Add the garlic and continue to sauté until the mixture is lightly browned. Transfer the mixture to a food processor or blender along with about half of the beans. Process until smoothly pureed.

Transfer the puree to a soup pot along with the remaining beans; the liquid, stock, or water; wine; parsley; dill; and curry powder or garam masala. Bring to a gentle simmer, then simmer very gently, covered, for 20 minutes.

In the meantime, cut the zucchini lengthwise into quarters, then into ¼-inch-thick slices. Heat the remaining oil in the skillet. Add the zucchini and water and sauté over medium heat, stirring frequently, until some of the pieces are lightly touched with brown. Stir into the soup. Adjust the consistency with more liquid if too thick. Season to taste with lemon juice, salt, and pepper and simmer for another 10 minutes over very low heat. If time allows, let the soup stand off the heat for at least an hour, then heat through before serving.

Calories: 171	Total fat: 3 g	Protein: 8 g
Carbohydrate: 25 g	Cholesterol: 0 g	Sodium: 5 mg

If pale beans bubble for you in a red earthenware pot, you can often decline the dinners of sumptuous hosts.

— Martial (c. A.D. 40–104)
Epigrams

Southeast Asian-Style Vegetable Stew

Serves 6 to 8

A one-dish meal enveloped in the rich flavor of peanut butter and spiced with chili peppers.

1 large leek, chopped and rinsed
8 ounces fresh slender string beans, trimmed and cut in half
½ cup water
3 cloves garlic, minced
1 to 2 fresh chilies, to taste, seeded and minced (see note)
3 cups broccoli florets
1 large red bell pepper, cut into narrow 2-inch strips
½ small head cauliflower, chopped into bite-sized pieces
4 to 6 ounces rice-stick noodles or other thin pasta such as angel-hair or vermicelli

Sauce:
Juice of 1 lime
½ cup reduced-fat peanut butter
2 tablespoons brown sugar
3 tablespoons soy sauce or tamari
2½ teaspoons cornstarch
1½ cups water

Garnishes (optional):
Chopped peanuts
Sliced scallions

Combine the leek and string beans with the water in a soup pot or large steep-sided wok and bring to a simmer. Cover and cook over medium heat about 4 to 8 minutes, or until the string beans are bright green. Stir in the garlic and chili or chilies, then layer the broccoli, bell pepper, and cauliflower into the pot or wok without stirring them in. Cover and cook for 8 to 10 minutes, or until all the vegetables are crisp-tender.

In the meantime, cook the rice-stick noodles or pasta until al dente, then drain.

Combine all the ingredients for the sauce in a food processor or blender and process until smooth. Add to the vegetable mixture in the pot and stir together. Bring to a gentle simmer and cook for another 5 to 10 minutes, uncovered, or until the sauce has thickened and the vegetables are just a bit softer than crisp-tender.

Place a small amount of noodles in the bottom of each serving bowl and ladle some of the stew over them. If you wish, garnish with chopped peanuts, sliced scallions, or both.

Note: Red pepper flakes may be substituted for fresh chilies. Add once all the vegetables are in the pot. Start with ½ teaspoon and add more to taste if you want a spicier effect.

Calories: 250	Total fat: 7 g	Protein: 7 g
Carbohydrate: 36 g	Cholesterol: 0 g	Sodium: 532 mg

Tomato-Rice Soup with Snow Peas

6 to 8 servings

Crisp green snow peas lend this soup a pleasant visual and textural twist.

2 tablespoons canola oil
1 large onion, chopped
4 cups water
⅔ cup raw brown rice, rinsed
2 large celery stalks, diced
1 28-ounce can tomato puree
2 bay leaves
2 teaspoons Italian herb mix
1 heaping cup sliced mushrooms
3 to 4 tablespoons chopped fresh parsley
Salt and freshly ground pepper to taste
6 ounces snow peas, trimmed and cut
    into 1-inch pieces

Heat the oil in a soup pot. Add the onion and sauté over medium heat until golden. Add the water, rice, celery, tomato puree, bay leaves, and herb mix. Bring to a simmer, then simmer gently, covered, until the rice is just done, about 40 to 45 minutes.

Add the mushrooms and parsley and adjust the consistency with more water if too thick. Simmer over low heat for another 15 minutes. Season to taste with salt and pepper.

If time allows, let the soup stand for an hour or so before serving, then heat through as needed. Just before serving, steam the snow peas until bright green and crisp-tender. After ladling the soup into bowls, garnish each serving with some snow peas.

| Calories: 142 | Total fat: 3 g | Protein: 3 g |
| Carbohydrate: 23 g | Cholesterol: 0 g | Sodium: 62 mg |

Okra-Rice Gumbo

6 to 8 servings

This classic from the American South contains a wonderfully diverse blend of flavors and textures, all pulled together by the unique character of okra. Serve with fresh Buttermilk Oat Muffins (page 141).

2 tablespoons canola oil
2 medium onions, chopped
2 medium celery stalks, diced
5 cups water
1 14- to 16-ounce can diced tomatoes, undrained
4 cups small, tender okra, sliced ½-inch thick
1 medium green bell pepper, chopped
⅔ cup raw brown rice, rinsed
2 bay leaves
1½ teaspoons salt-free herb-and-spice seasoning mix
¼ teaspoon dried red pepper flakes or cayenne pepper, or to taste
Salt and freshly ground pepper to taste

Heat the oil in a soup pot. Add the onions and celery and sauté over low heat until the onions are golden. Add the water and all the remaining ingredients except the salt and pepper. Enough red pepper flakes or cayenne should be used to give the soup a distinct bite, but use your discretion. Bring to a simmer, then simmer gently, covered, stirring occasionally, for about an hour, or until the rice is cooked and the vegetables are tender. Season to taste with salt and pepper.

Serve at once, or let the soup stand for an hour or so, then heat through as needed. The soup will thicken considerably as it stands. Adjust the consistency with more water as needed and correct the seasonings, but let it remain very thick, with the consistency of a stew.

| Calories: 118 | Total fat: 3 g | Protein: 3 g |
| Carbohydrate: 17 g | Cholesterol: 0 g | Sodium: 21 mg |

The great dish of New Orleans, and which it claims the honor of having invented, is the Gumbo. There is no dish which at the same time so tickles the palate, satisfies the appetite, furnishes the body with nutriment sufficient to carry on the physical requirements, and costs so little, as the Creole Gumbo. It is a dinner in itself, being soup, pièce de résistance and vegetable in one. Healthy, not heating to the stomach, and easy of digestion, it should grace every table.

— William Coleman, 1885

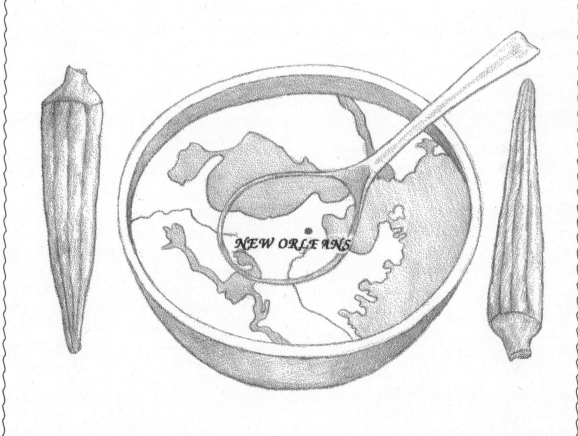

Cream of Broccoli Soup with Whole Wheat Pasta

6 or more servings

2 large bunches broccoli
2 tablespoons soy margarine, divided
2 tablespoons water
2 medium onions, chopped
2 cloves garlic, minced
1 large celery stalk, diced
2 tablespoons unbleached white flour
1 large tomato, chopped
¼ cup firmly packed chopped fresh parsley
2 teaspoons salt-free herb-and-spice
    seasoning mix
Light Vegetable Stock (page 7) or water,
    as needed
2 cups low-fat milk or soy milk, or as needed
1 cup small whole wheat shell or elbow pasta
Salt and freshly ground pepper to taste
Grated Parmesan cheese or
    Parmesan–style soy cheese for topping,
    optional

Finely chop the broccoli, then set aside about 1½ cups of the florets.

Heat 1 tablespoon of the margarine in a large soup pot along with 2 tablespoons of water. Add the onions, garlic, and celery and sauté over medium heat until the onions are golden. Slowly sprinkle in the flour, stirring it in until it disappears.

Add the chopped broccoli (except for the reserved florets), tomato, parsley, seasoning mix, and just enough stock or water to cover. Bring to a simmer, then simmer gently, covered, for 15 to 20 minutes, or until the broccoli is tender but not overdone. Remove from the heat.

Transfer the solid ingredients with a slotted spoon to a food processor or blender and puree, in batches if necessary, until smooth. Stir back into the stock in the soup pot and add enough milk or soy milk to achieve a smooth and slightly thick consistency. Return to very low heat.

Cook the pasta in a separate saucepan in rapidly simmering water until it is al dente. Drain and rinse briefly under cool water. In the meantime, steam the broccoli florets until they are bright green and crisp-tender.

Heat the remaining tablespoon of margarine in a skillet. Sauté the pasta over medium heat until it just begins to brown lightly. Stir the pasta and the steamed florets into the soup, then season to taste with salt and pepper. Let the soup remain on very low heat for another 5 minutes, then serve, garnishing each serving with some grated cheese if desired.

Calories: 246	Total fat: 5 g	Protein: 10 g
Carbohydrate: 39 g	Cholesterol: 3 g	Sodium: 145 mg

Potage Maigre
(Lettuce, Cucumber, and Fresh Pea Soup)

6 to 8 servings

This light soup of lettuce, cucumber, and fresh spring peas was quite common in nineteenth-century America. *Potage maigre* translates loosely as a Fast-Day soup, traditionally made for Lent. Versions of it appear in old Creole and Pennsylvania Dutch cookbooks.

2 tablespoons canola oil
2 large onions, quartered and thinly sliced
1 large celery stalk, finely diced
Handful of celery leaves
2 small heads Boston or Bibb lettuce, finely shredded
5 cups Light Vegetable Stock (page 7) or water with 2 vegetable bouillon cubes
1 cup steamed fresh green peas
1 cup peeled, grated, and seeded cucumber
¼ cup chopped fresh parsley
2 tablespoons chopped fresh dill
Salt and freshly ground pepper to taste
Parsley-Potato Dumplings (page 153), optional
Reduced-fat sour cream or plain low-fat yogurt, optional

Heat the oil in a soup pot. Add the onions and sauté over moderately low heat until they are translucent. Add the diced celery and continue to sauté until the onions begin to turn golden. Add the celery leaves, lettuce, and stock or water. Bring to a simmer, then simmer gently, covered, for 10 to 15 minutes, or until the lettuce is wilted but still has a bit of crunch.

Add the peas and cucumber. Adjust the consistency with a bit more stock or water if the vegetables seem crowded. Stir in the parsley and dill, then season to taste with salt and lots of freshly ground pepper. Simmer over very low heat for another 10 minutes.

Serve hot with Parsley-Potato Dumplings if desired, and/or cool to room temperature and top each serving with a dollop of sour cream or yogurt.

Calories: 119	Total fat: 3 g	Protein: 3 g
Carbohydrate: 17 g	Cholesterol: 0 g	Sodium: 33 mg

Chinese Cabbage and Bean Curd Soup

4 to 6 servings

This light soup, served with Scallion Logs (page 147), is a great introduction to an Oriental-style vegetable stir-fry with rice or noodles.

1 tablespoon canola oil

1 large onion, quartered and thinly sliced

2 cups firmly packed, finely shredded
 savoy cabbage

¾ cup thinly sliced small white mushrooms

6-ounce can sliced water chestnuts,
 undrained

1 recipe Onion or Leek and Garlic Broth
 (page 8) or Oriental Mushroom Broth
 (page 11)

2 tablespoons dry sherry or wine

2 teaspoons soy sauce or tamari

½ teaspoon lemon-pepper

1 cup snow peas, trimmed and halved

8 ounces tofu, cut into ½-inch dice

Heat the oil in a large soup pot. Add the onion and sauté over low heat until golden. Add the remaining ingredients, except the snow peas and tofu. Bring to a simmer, then simmer, covered, over low heat for 10 minutes.

Remove from the heat. Stir in the snow peas and tofu and let the soup stand for 30 minutes. Heat through as needed and serve at once.

Calories: 155	Total fat: 6 g	Protein: 5 g
Carbohydrate: 15 g	Cholesterol: 0 g	Sodium: 173 mg

To make nutritious, healthful, and palatable soup, with flavors properly commingled, is an art which requires study and practice, but it is surprising from what a scant allotment of material a delicate and appetizing dish may be produced.

— *The Buckeye Cookbook,* 1883

Miso-Spinach Soup with Baby Corn

4 to 6 servings

Simple, quick, and colorful, this soup is best eaten as soon as it is done. It makes a nice introduction to an Oriental rice or noodle dish. For more information on miso, see page 9, under Simple Miso Broth.

1 tablespoon canola or peanut oil

1 medium carrot, peeled and coarsely chopped

½ pound fresh spinach, washed, stemmed, and coarsely chopped

3 scallions, white and green parts, sliced

1 recipe Basic Dashi (page 10), Light Vegetable Stock (page 7), or 5 cups water

2 to 3 tablespoons sherry or dry wine

¼ teaspoon lemon-pepper

4 ounces tofu, cut into ½-inch dice

1 15- or 16-ounce can baby corn, cut into 1-inch pieces, liquid reserved

2 to 4 tablespoons miso, to taste

Heat the oil in a soup pot. Add the carrot and sauté over moderate heat for 2 minutes, stirring frequently. Add the spinach; scallions; dashi, stock, or water; sherry or wine; and lemon-pepper. Bring to a simmer, then simmer very gently, covered, for 10 minutes. Add the tofu and baby corn with its liquid.

Dissolve the miso in enough water to make it smooth and pourable. Stir it in and simmer for another 5 minutes over very low heat. Serve at once.

Calories: 155	Total fat: 4 g	Protein: 5 g
Carbohydrate: 21 g	Cholesterol: 0 g	Sodium: 113 mg

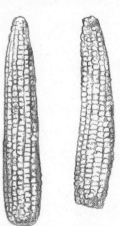

Egg Drop-Noodle Soup with Exotic Mushrooms

6 servings

This Oriental-style soup is a treat for those who love unusual mushrooms. Scallion Logs (page 147) are a good accompaniment. This is a perfect introduction to a simple meal of stir-fried vegetables with tofu.

2 teaspoons sesame oil
1 clove garlic, minced
4 scallions, white and green parts, sliced
1 recipe Oriental Mushroom Broth (page 11) with trimmed shiitake mushrooms
1 15- or 16-ounce can Oriental mushrooms, such as straw, abalone, or oyster mushrooms (leave straw mushrooms whole; coarsely chop abalone or oyster), undrained
1 6-ounce can sliced water chestnuts, undrained
1 tablespoon rice vinegar
1 tablespoon cornstarch
4 ounces rice-stick noodles
Soy sauce or tamari to taste
Freshly ground pepper to taste
2 eggs, beaten

Heat the oil in a soup pot, then add the garlic and white parts of the scallions and sauté over moderate heat for 2 or 3 minutes. Add the green parts of the scallions along with the broth, mushrooms, water chestnuts, and rice vinegar. Bring to a simmer, then simmer gently, covered, for 10 minutes.

Dissolve the cornstarch in just enough water to make it pourable and stir into the soup. Break up the rice-stick noodles and add them to the soup. Simmer for 5 minutes, or until the rice noodles are done.

Season to taste with soy sauce or tamari and freshly ground pepper, and adjust the consistency with water if the soup needs a bit more liquid. Pour the eggs into the soup in a thin, steady stream. Remove from the heat and serve at once.

Calories: 177	Total fat: 5 g	Protein: 4 g
Carbohydrate: 28 g	Cholesterol: 71 g	Sodium: 190 mg

Parsley-Potato Soup

6 to 8 servings

Lots of fresh parsley and a touch of cream cheese give this soup its special character. Serve with crusty French or Italian bread.

1 tablespoon canola oil
1 large onion, chopped
2 cloves garlic, minced
6 medium potatoes, peeled and diced
2 bay leaves
Light Vegetable Stock (page 7) or water,
    as needed
1 teaspoon Italian herb mix
4 ounces low-fat cream cheese, diced
½ cup firmly packed chopped fresh parsley
¼ cup quick-cooking oats
1 cup low-fat milk, or as needed
Salt and freshly ground pepper to taste

Heat the oil in a soup pot. Add the onion and sauté over medium heat until golden. Add the garlic, potatoes, and bay leaves. Add enough stock or water to cover, then stir in the herb mix. Bring to a simmer, then simmer gently, covered, until the potatoes are just tender, about 20 to 25 minutes.

Remove about ½ cup of the hot liquid with a ladle and transfer it to a small mixing bowl. Combine with the cream cheese and whisk together until smooth and creamy. Stir into the soup along with the parsley. Slowly sprinkle in the oats. Simmer for another 20 to 25 minutes over very low heat, or until the potatoes are completely tender. Add the milk and season to taste with salt and pepper.

This soup thickens as it stands; thin as needed with additional milk, then correct the seasonings.

Calories: 236   Total fat: 7 g   Protein: 6 g
Carbohydrate: 38 g   Cholesterol: 16 g   Sodium: 113 mg

S·U·M·M·E·R

When the appetite is dulled by summer's heat, nothing is more appealing than a bowl of refreshing cold soup. These soups make lavish use of herbs, garden vegetables, and lush fruits. For really lazy, languid days, you'll find a number of soups that require no cooking at all.

Cream of Green Pea and Cucumber Soup

6 servings

This brightly colored soup makes a delightful introduction to a summer meal, or it can be the mainstay of a light meal accompanied by fresh bread and a bountiful salad.

1 cup chopped onion

3 cloves garlic, minced

2 large potatoes, peeled and diced

1 large cucumber, peeled, seeded, and coarsely chopped

4 cups water

2 cups frozen green peas, thawed

¼ cup chopped fresh parsley

2 tablespoons chopped fresh dill

2 cups low-fat milk or soy milk, or as needed

Juice of ½ to 1 lemon, to taste

Salt and freshly ground pepper to taste

1 cup fresh green peas, lightly steamed

1 cup peeled, seeded, and finely diced cucumber

Combine the onion, garlic, potatoes, and cucumber in a soup pot with the water and bring to a simmer. Simmer gently, covered, until the vegetables are tender, about 25 minutes. Transfer the solid ingredients to a food processor or blender along with the peas, parsley, and dill. Process until very smoothly pureed, then transfer back to the soup pot.

Stir in enough milk or soy milk to achieve a slightly thick consistency. Add lemon juice, salt, and pepper to taste.

Let the soup cool to room temperature, then stir in the steamed fresh peas and additional cucumber. Serve at room temperature or refrigerate for an hour or two and serve chilled.

Calories: 166	Total fat: 1 g	Protein: 8 g
Carbohydrate: 31 g	Cholesterol: 3 g	Sodium: 50 mg

Young green peas! Do not these words sound pleasant to the ear...I fancy that, by merely raising my eyes from the paper on which I am now writing, I shall see all our garden in bud and blossom.

— Alexia Soyer
The Modern Housewife, 1851

Cool Ratatouille

6 to 8 servings

This summery version of the classic stew makes use of summer's lush tomatoes and fresh herbs. Serve with Bruschetta (page 150).

2 tablespoons olive oil
1 large onion, chopped
3 to 4 cloves garlic, minced
2 medium eggplants (about 1½ pounds total), peeled and diced
2 small zucchini, sliced
4 cups diced ripe, juicy, fresh tomatoes
1½ cups sliced mushrooms
1 cup tomato sauce
¼ cup dry red wine
1 teaspoon paprika
¾ cup water
¼ cup chopped fresh parsley
2 tablespoons chopped fresh basil
1 teaspoon chopped fresh oregano
1 teaspoon fresh thyme leaves, optional
Salt and freshly ground pepper to taste
Reduced-fat sour cream or low-fat yogurt for topping, optional
Thinly sliced green or purple basil for garnish, optional

Heat the oil in a large soup pot. Add the onion and garlic and sauté over medium heat until golden, about 8 to 10 minutes. Add the eggplants, zucchini, tomatoes, mushrooms, tomato sauce, wine, paprika, and the water. Bring to a simmer and cook over medium heat, covered, until the vegetables are tender but not overdone, about 25 to 30 minutes. Stir occasionally, making sure there is enough liquid for the vegetables to simmer in without being too soupy. Add small amounts of water if needed.

Remove from the heat and stir in the fresh herbs. Season with salt and pepper. Let the stew cool to room temperature.

Serve in bowls with a dollop of sour cream or yogurt and a few strips of basil leaf if desired.

| Calories: 136 | Total fat: 4 g | Protein: 2 g |
| Carbohydrate: 20 g | Cholesterol: 0 g | Sodium: 230 mg |

Summer Pasta Soup

6 to 8 servings

This garden-fresh soup is a good choice when you want a summery soup that is slightly warm rather than chilled.

5 cups Light Vegetable Stock (page 7) or water with 2 vegetable bouillon cubes

2 pounds ripe tomatoes, diced

2 medium-small zucchini, quartered lengthwise and sliced

3 to 4 scallions, sliced

1 16-ounce can small white beans, drained and rinsed

¼ to ½ cup chopped fresh parsley, to taste

Salt and freshly ground pepper to taste

3 cups uncooked bow tie pasta (about 6 ounces)

8 to 10 basil leaves, thinly sliced

Grated Parmesan cheese or soy Parmesan for topping, optional

Combine the stock or water in a large soup pot with the tomatoes, zucchini, and scallions. Bring to a simmer, then simmer gently, covered, until the zucchini is tender but still firm, about 10 minutes.

Add the beans and parsley, then season to taste with salt and pepper. Remove from the heat and let the soup stand, covered, for an hour or so before serving. This will give it time to cool somewhat as well as to develop flavor.

About 20 minutes before the soup is to be served, bring water to boil in a separate large pot and cook the pasta until it is al dente. Drain and rinse briefly with cool water to stop the cooking process, then stir into the soup.

Serve the soup just warm, topping each serving with a few strips of basil leaf and, if desired, a sprinkling of Parmesan cheese or soy Parmesan.

Calories: 170	Total fat: 0 g	Protein: 7 g
Carbohydrate: 34 g	Cholesterol: 0 g	Sodium: 35 mg

Potato-Spinach Buttermilk Soup

6 to 8 servings

A cold soup that is substantial as well as refreshing. Serve with a fresh, purchased rye bread.

5 to 6 medium potatoes, peeled and diced
1 small onion, cut in half
2 bay leaves
Light Vegetable Stock (page 7) or water,
    as needed
1 pound fresh spinach leaves, well
    washed, stemmed, and chopped
1 cup steamed fresh or thawed frozen
    green peas
2 to 2½ cups buttermilk, as needed
2 to 3 tablespoons chopped fresh parsley
1 tablespoon minced fresh dill
Salt and freshly ground pepper to taste

Combine the potatoes, onion, and bay leaves in a large soup pot with just enough stock or water to cover. Bring to a simmer, then simmer gently, covered, until the potatoes are tender, about 25 minutes. Remove from the heat. With a slotted spoon, remove and discard onion halves.

With a slotted spoon, transfer 1 heaping cup of the potato dice into a small bowl, mash well, and stir back into the soup. Stir in the spinach leaves and allow the soup to cool to room temperature. Stir in the remaining ingredients and season to taste with salt and pepper. Chill thoroughly before serving.

Calories: 209	Total fat: 0 g	Protein: 8 g
Carbohydrate: 42 g	Cholesterol: 3 g	Sodium: 119 mg

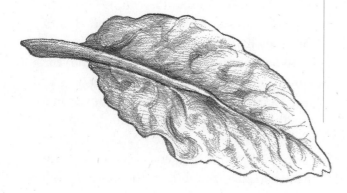

Cool Cream of Potato Soup with Leeks and Greens

6 to 8 servings

A lightly curried soup that combines the mildness of potatoes with the earthy goodness of sharp greens. Make sure to rinse the leeks and the greens very thoroughly — even a small amount of grit can ruin a good soup!

6 medium potatoes, peeled and diced
2 medium onions, chopped
2 cloves garlic, minced
1 tablespoon canola oil
2 tablespoons water
2 to 3 medium leeks, white and palest green parts only, chopped and rinsed
½ cup finely diced red bell pepper
1 medium head escarole, chicory, or arugula, cut into coarse shreds
1 cup reduced-fat sour cream or plain low-fat yogurt
2 cups low-fat milk
2 tablespoons minced fresh dill, optional
1 to 2 teaspoons good quality curry powder or garam masala, to taste
Salt to taste

Combine the potatoes, onions, and garlic in a large soup pot with enough water to cover. Bring to a simmer, then simmer gently, covered, until the potatoes are quite tender, about 25 minutes. Remove from the heat and let cool to room temperature.

About an hour or two before serving, heat the oil in a wide skillet with the water. Add the leeks and "sweat" them, covered, for 5 to 10 minutes, or until wilted, stirring occasionally. Add the red pepper and greens, then cover and steam until the greens are tender, stirring occasionally. This will take from 5 to 10 minutes or slightly more, depending on the variety of the greens and the thickness of the leaves. Add a bit more water if necessary to prevent sticking.

While the greens are steaming, transfer the potato-onion mixture, with its liquid, to a food processor or blender and puree until smooth. Return to the soup pot. Once the leeks and greens are done, stir them into the soup pot. Stir in the sour cream or yogurt and the milk. If the soup is too dense, add a small amount of water. It should have a medium-thick consistency. Season to taste with fresh dill if desired, curry powder or garam masala, and salt, then cover and chill for an hour or two before serving.

Calories: 244	Total fat: 7 g	Protein: 6 g
Carbohydrate: 38 g	Cholesterol: 5 g	Sodium: 72 mg

As long as you have eaten the strong-smelling shoots of Tarentine leeks, give kisses with shut mouth.

— Martial (c. A.D. 40 –104)
   Epigrams

Garden Greens Soup

6 servings

A summer soup that looks and tastes garden fresh.

1½ tablespoons canola oil
2 medium onions, quartered and thinly
    sliced
1 large celery stalk, finely diced
½ small head savoy cabbage, finely
    shredded
5 cups Light Vegetable Stock (page 7)
    or 5 cups water with 2 vegetable
    bouillon cubes
¼ cup quick-cooking oatmeal
12 ounces fresh, triple-washed spinach,
    lightly rinsed, stemmed, and chopped
2 cups shredded lettuce, any dark green
    variety
2 medium tomatoes, finely diced
¼ cup chopped fresh parsley
2 tablespoons minced fresh dill
2 bunches scallions, thinly sliced
½ teaspoon good quality curry powder
    or garam masala
1½ cups buttermilk, or as needed
Salt and freshly ground pepper to taste

Heat the oil in a large soup pot. Add the onion and celery and sauté over medium heat until the onion is golden. Add the cabbage, stock or water, and oatmeal. Bring to a simmer, then simmer gently, covered, for 10 minutes. Add the spinach, lettuce, tomatoes, parsley, dill, scallions, and curry powder or garam masala. Simmer over low heat for 10 minutes more, then remove from the heat. Allow the soup to cool to room temperature.

Stir in the buttermilk as needed to achieve a slightly thick consistency. Season to taste with salt and pepper. Refrigerate the soup for an hour or so before serving.

Calories: 154	Total fat: 4 g	Protein: 6 g
Carbohydrate: 22 g	Cholesterol: 2 g	Sodium: 115 mg

Cream of Lettuce Soup

6 servings

Cheddar-Oat Griddle Biscuits (page 143) provide a nice contrast to the mild flavor of this pleasant summer soup.

1½ tablespoons canola oil
2 medium onions, chopped
3 to 4 cloves garlic, minced
2½ cups water
10 cups coarsely chopped lettuce, divided
1 cup low-fat milk
Juice of ½ lemon
¼ cup minced fresh herbs (choose from a mixture of chives, dill, oregano, basil)
⅔ cup plain low-fat yogurt or reduced-fat sour cream
Salt and lemon-pepper to taste

Because lettuces are owned by the moon, they cool and moisten what heat and dryness Mars causeth.

— Nicolas Culpeper
The Complete Herbal, 1653

Heat the oil in a soup pot. Add the onions and garlic and sauté over moderate heat until the onions are lightly browned. Add the water and 8 cups of the lettuce, reserving the rest. Bring to a simmer, then simmer gently, covered, for 20 minutes. With a slotted spoon, transfer the solid ingredients to a food processor or blender and puree, in batches if necessary, until smooth.

Return to the soup pot or to a serving tureen. Stir in the milk, lemon juice, and herbs. Allow to cool to room temperature.

Stir in the yogurt or sour cream and add a bit more milk if the soup is too thick. Season to taste with salt and lemon-pepper.

Finely shred the reserved lettuce and place it in a saucepan with about a half inch of water. Steam, covered, just until wilted. Stir into the soup. Refrigerate the soup for at least an hour before serving. This soup is best served the same day it is made.

Calories: 90	Total fat: 4 g	Protein: 3 g
Carbohydrate: 9 g	Cholesterol: 3 g	Sodium: 45 mg

Middle Eastern Cucumber-Yogurt Soup

4 to 6 servings

Here's an exceptionally easy no-cook soup — a classic from the Middle East. I enjoy it with barley added, as suggested in the variation below.

2 large cucumbers, peeled and seeded
1 pint plain yogurt
¼ cup finely chopped mixed fresh herbs
    (such as dill, parsley, and mint), or
    more to taste
1½ cups low-fat milk, or as needed
1 teaspoon granulated sugar
½ teaspoon ground cumin
Salt and freshly ground pepper to taste
Juice of ½ lemon, optional

Grate the cucumbers on a coarse grater, then place them in a colander. Place the colander over the container in which you will serve the soup. Salt the grated cucumbers lightly and let stand for 30 minutes. The juice from the cucumbers will drain into the container, and the cucumbers themselves will become pleasantly crisp.

Place the cucumbers in the container with the cucumber juice. Stir in the yogurt, herbs, and enough milk to give a slightly thick consistency. Stir in the sugar and seasonings, then add the optional lemon juice if you'd like an extra tangy flavor. Serve at once or refrigerate until needed.

Variation: For a heartier version of this soup, add a cup or so of cold cooked barley.

Calories: 114	Total fat: 2 g	Protein: 9 g
Carbohydrate: 15 g	Cholesterol: 9 g	Sodium: 112 mg

Cold Zucchini and Corn Soup

6 to 8 servings

Zucchini and corn are an appealing team. Serve with Garlic Croutons (page 149) to add a pleasant crunch.

2 tablespoons olive oil, divided
1 small onion, chopped
1 clove garlic, minced
2 pounds zucchini, diced, divided
2 cups cooked fresh corn kernels (from about 3 good-sized ears), divided
¼ cup chopped fresh parsley
5 cups Light Vegetable Stock (page 7) or water
1 teaspoon ground cumin
2 scallions, green parts only, minced
2 tablespoons finely chopped fresh basil
1 cup low-fat sour cream
1 to 2 tablespoons lemon juice, to taste
Salt and freshly ground pepper to taste

Heat half of the oil in a soup pot. Add the onion and garlic and sauté over medium heat until the onion is golden. Set aside half of the zucchini dice and half of the corn kernels. Add the remaining halves to the soup pot along with the parsley, stock or water, and cumin. Bring to a simmer, then simmer gently, covered, until the zucchini is tender, about 10 minutes.

With a slotted spoon, transfer the solid ingredients to a food processor or blender and puree, in batches if necessary, until smooth. Return to the soup pot, then allow to cool to room temperature.

Heat the remaining olive oil in a skillet. Add the reserved zucchini and sauté over medium heat until it is just beginning to brown lightly. When the soup is cool, stir in the sautéed zucchini, reserved corn kernels, scallions, basil, sour cream, and lemon juice. Correct the consistency if necessary with additional stock or water, then season to taste with salt and freshly ground pepper. Serve at room temperature or refrigerate until chilled, as you prefer.

Calories: 186	Total fat: 8 g	Protein: 4 g
Carbohydrate: 23 g	Cholesterol: 2 g	Sodium: 43 mg

Cream of Corn and Watercress Soup

6 to 8 servings

The peppery flavor of watercress provides an excellent contrast to the sweetness of summer corn.

6 medium ears fresh sweet corn
2 tablespoons canola oil
2 large onions, chopped
2 cloves garlic, minced
2 medium potatoes, diced
4 cups cooking liquid from the corn
2 cups chopped watercress leaves
    and stems, divided
1 teaspoon Italian herb mix
2 cups low-fat milk or soy milk, or as
    needed
Salt and freshly ground pepper

Cook the corn in plenty of rapidly simmering water until the kernels are just tender, then remove the corn with tongs and reserve the water. When the corn is cool enough to handle, scrape the kernels off the cobs with a sharp knife. Set the kernels aside.

Heat the oil in a soup pot. Add the onion and garlic and sauté over medium heat until golden. Add the potatoes and cooking liquid from the corn and bring to a simmer. Simmer gently, covered, for 10 minutes. Add half of the watercress along with the herb mix. Simmer until the potatoes are tender, about 10 to 15 minutes more, then remove from the heat.

Set aside 1 cup of the corn kernels and puree the remainder in a food processor or blender until fairly smooth. Transfer to a bowl. With a slotted spoon, transfer the solid ingredients from the soup to the food processor or blender and puree until smooth. Return the puree to the soup pot, along with the corn puree, the reserved corn kernels, and the reserved watercress.

Return to low heat and stir in enough milk or soy milk to achieve a slightly thick consistency. Season to taste with salt and pepper, then cover and simmer over low heat for another 10 to 15 minutes. Let the soup cool to room temperature, then refrigerate until chilled.

Calories: 165	Total fat: 5 g	Protein: 5 g
Carbohydrate: 25 g	Cholesterol: 3 g	Sodium: 45 mg

"Eat well of the cresses" was a common bit of advice given by Renaissance herbalists, for it was believed that consuming these greens aided the memory.

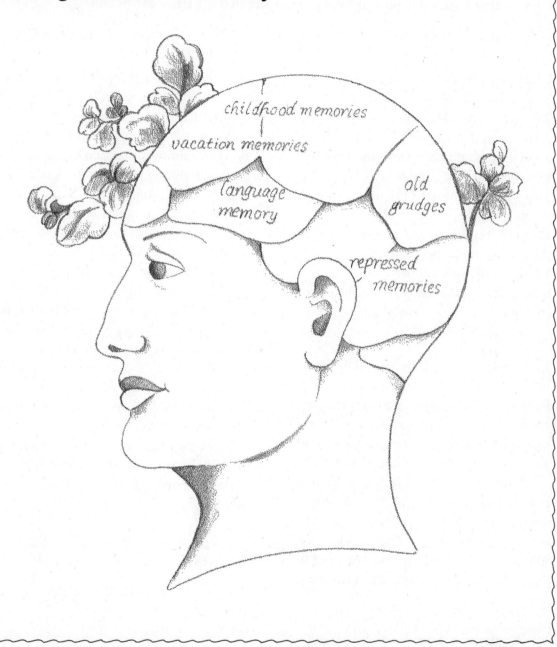

Creamy Corn Soup with Roasted Peppers

6 servings

An appetizing soup designed to impress your summer guests — or yourself!

6 large ears fresh sweet corn
2 tablespoons canola oil, divided
2 large onions, chopped
2 cloves garlic, minced
4 cups cooking liquid from the corn
Pinch of cayenne pepper
1 to 1½ cups low-fat milk or soy milk,
    as needed
Salt and freshly ground pepper to taste
2 large sweet red bell peppers
1 large green bell pepper
6 large fresh basil leaves, sliced into strips,
    optional

Cook the corn in plenty of rapidly simmering water until the kernels are just tender. Remove the corn with tongs and reserve the cooking water. When the corn is cool enough to handle, scrape the kernels off the cobs with a sharp knife. Set aside 1 cup of kernels.

Meanwhile, heat half of the oil in a soup pot. Add the onions and garlic and sauté over medium heat until the onions are golden and just beginning to be touched with brown spots. Transfer the onions and garlic to a food processor or blender and process with the corn kernels (except for the reserved cup), in batches if necessary, until smoothly pureed. Transfer back to the soup pot.

Stir in the cooking liquid from the corn. Bring to a simmer, then add the cayenne pepper and enough milk or soy milk to achieve a slightly thick consistency. Simmer gently, covered, for 10 minutes. Season to taste with salt and pepper. Allow the soup to stand off the heat, uncovered, for about an hour.

In the meantime, set the peppers under the broiler, turning them frequently until the skins are quite blistered and fairly charred. Place the peppers in a brown paper bag and fold shut. Let the peppers cool in the bag for 30 minutes or so, then remove them from the bag, slip the skins off, and remove stems and seeds. Cut the peppers into narrow strips.

Serve the soup just warm or at room temperature, garnishing each serving with some roasted pepper strips and basil leaves if desired.

| Calories: 222 | Total fat: 5 g | Protein: 5 g |
| Carbohydrate: 38 g | Cholesterol: 2 g | Sodium: 36 mg |

Fresh Tomato Soup with Sweet Corn Sauce

6 servings

This unusual cold soup is quite elegant and as appealing to look at as it is to eat.

2 pounds ripe, flavorful tomatoes
2 tablespoons olive oil
2 large onions, chopped
2 cloves garlic, minced
2 large celery stalks, diced
1 medium potato, scrubbed and finely diced
2 cups water
¼ cup chopped fresh basil
2 tablespoons chopped fresh dill
1 teaspoon salt-free herb-and-spice
    seasoning mix
4 ears fresh corn
½ cup reduced-fat sour cream or plain
    low-fat yogurt
1½ to 2 cups tomato juice, as needed
1 tablespoon lemon juice
Salt and freshly ground pepper to taste
Chopped fresh basil for garnish

Bring about 2 quarts of water to a boil in a large saucepan. Place the whole tomatoes in the boiling water, remove the pot from the heat, and let stand for 1 minute. Remove the tomatoes and when they are cool enough to handle, peel them. Chop and set aside.

Heat the oil in a soup pot. Add the onions, garlic, and celery and sauté over medium heat, stirring frequently, until the onion is golden. Add the potato, the chopped tomatoes, and water. Bring to a simmer, then simmer gently, covered, until the potato is tender, about 20 minutes. Add the basil, dill, and seasoning mix and simmer for another 5 minutes. Remove from the heat and allow to cool to room temperature.

In the meantime, cook the corn until just tender, then drain and allow it to cool. When the corn is cool enough to handle, scrape the kernels off the cobs with a sharp knife. Combine the corn kernels with the sour cream or yogurt in a food processor or blender and puree until very smooth. Place in a container and refrigerate until needed.

Once the tomato mixture has cooled, puree it in batches in a food processor or blender until well pureed. Return it to the soup pot and add enough tomato juice to achieve a slightly thick consistency. Stir in the lemon juice and season to taste with salt and pepper. Refrigerate until chilled.

To serve, fill each serving bowl about three quarters full with the tomato soup. Place a ladleful of the sweet corn sauce in the center of each bowl and garnish each serving with a sprinkling of chopped basil.

| Calories: 191 | Total fat: 8 g | Protein: 4 g |
| Carbohydrate: 27 g | Cholesterol: 1 g | Sodium: 44 mg |

Carrot-Yogurt Soup with Broccoli

6 to 8 servings

2 tablespoons canola oil
2 large onions, chopped
1 pound carrots, peeled and finely diced
1 large potato, peeled and finely diced
2 large celery stalks, finely diced
2 large ripe tomatoes, chopped
2 bay leaves
2 teaspoons salt-free herb-and-spice
    seasoning mix
1 large bunch broccoli, finely chopped
1 cup plain low-fat yogurt
1 cup low-fat milk, or as needed
3 to 4 tablespoons minced fresh dill
½ teaspoon lemon-pepper
Salt to taste

Heat the oil in a soup pot. Add the onions and sauté over medium heat until golden. Add the carrots, potato, celery, and tomatoes. Add just enough water to cover, then stir in the bay leaves and seasoning mix. Bring to a simmer, then simmer gently, covered, until all the vegetables are tender, about 25 minutes. Allow the soup to cool to room temperature. Puree the soup, in batches if necessary, in a food processor or blender.

Steam the broccoli in a large saucepan with about an inch of water until bright green and crisp-tender. Drain in a colander and rinse briefly with cool water to stop the cooking process. Stir the broccoli into the soup followed by the yogurt and enough milk to achieve a slightly thick consistency.

Stir in the dill and lemon-pepper and season to taste with salt. Let the soup cool to room temperature, then refrigerate until chilled.

Calories: 155	Total fat: 5 g	Protein: 5 g
Carbohydrate: 22 g	Cholesterol: 4 g	Sodium: 113 mg

To dream of carrots signifies strength and profit to them that are at law for an inheritance, for we pluck them out of the ground with our hand.

— Richard Folkard
    Plant Lore, Legends and Lyrics, 1884

Quick Cool Pinto Bean Puree

6 servings

With the help of a food processor, this tasty, no-cook soup will be ready to eat in minutes. Serve with low-fat tortilla chips or warmed flour tortillas.

2 1-pound cans pinto beans, drained and rinsed

1 14- to 16-ounce can stewed or diced tomatoes, undrained

2 scallions, coarsely chopped

¼ cup fresh cilantro or parsley leaves

Juice of 1 lemon

1 teaspoon chili powder

1 teaspoon ground cumin

1 medium green bell pepper, cut into 1-inch pieces

4 ripe plum tomatoes, cut into large chunks

½ cup pitted black olives

¼ cup chopped mild green chilies (fresh or canned), optional

1½ cups Light Vegetable Stock (page 7) or water, or as needed

Combine the beans, canned tomatoes, scallions, and cilantro or parsley in a food processor or blender and process until well pureed. Transfer to a large serving container and stir in the lemon juice, chili powder, and cumin.

Place the green pepper and fresh tomatoes in the food processor and pulse on and off 2 or 3 times. Add the olives and pulse on and off quickly, 2 or 3 times more, or until the vegetables are finely chopped (approximately ¼-inch pieces). Take care not to overprocess. Stir into the bean puree, then add the chilies if desired.

Stir in enough stock or water to achieve a medium-thick consistency. Serve at once, or cover and refrigerate until needed.

Variation: Garnish each serving with diced avocado and extra scallions.

Calories: 211	Total fat: 2 g	Protein: 9 g
Carbohydrate: 37 g	Cholesterol: 0 g	Sodium: 100 mg

Creamy Avocado Soup

4 to 6 servings

A quick and easy no-cook soup, this is remarkably refreshing on a hot summer day. It's best eaten on the same day as it is made, since avocado discolors and does not keep well under refrigeration once cut. This soup makes a great opener for a Southwestern-style meal of burritos, enchiladas, and the like.

2 large ripe avocados, pitted and peeled
Juice of ½ lemon
1½ cups buttermilk
1½ cups low-fat milk, or as needed
1 medium green or red bell pepper, finely chopped
2 scallions, green parts only, thinly sliced
2 tablespoons finely chopped fresh dill
2 tablespoons finely chopped fresh parsley
½ teaspoon ground cumin
½ teaspoon good quality curry powder or garam masala
Salt and freshly ground pepper to taste

Finely dice enough avocado to make 1 cup, then mash the remaining avocado well. Combine the diced and mashed avocados in a serving container and mix immediately with the lemon juice. Stir in the buttermilk, then enough milk to achieve a slightly thick consistency. Stir in the remaining ingredients and refrigerate, covered, until thoroughly chilled.

| Calories: 209 | Total fat: 11 g | Protein: 7 g |
| Carbohydrate: 19 g | Cholesterol: 6 g | Sodium: 89 mg |

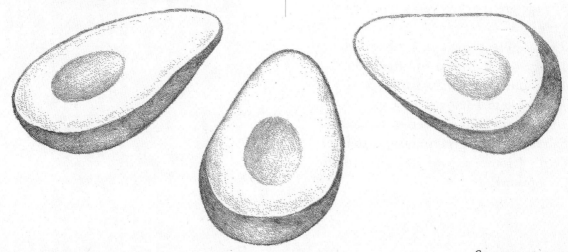

Gazpacho

6 servings

A collection of vegetarian soups wouldn't be complete without this Spanish classic.

The base:

1 14- to 16-ounce can diced or stewed
　tomatoes, undrained
⅔ large cucumber, peeled and cut into
　chunks
⅔ large green or red bell pepper, cut
　into chunks
2 bunches scallions, cut into several pieces
Handful of parsley sprigs
1 tablespoon chopped fresh dill or
　1 teaspoon dried dill

To finish the soup:

3 cups tomato juice, or as needed
⅓ large cucumber, peeled and finely
　diced
⅓ large green or red bell pepper, finely
　diced
2 fresh plum tomatoes, finely diced
1 large carrot, peeled and finely diced
1 medium celery stalk, finely diced
Juice of ½ to 1 lemon, to taste
2 teaspoons chili powder, or to taste
Salt and freshly ground pepper to taste
Garlic Croutons (page 149) for topping,
　optional

Place all the ingredients for the soup base in a food processor or blender. Puree until fairly smooth. Transfer the puree to a serving container. Stir in enough tomato juice to give the soup a slightly thick consistency. Add the remaining ingredients. Stir together, then cover and refrigerate for at least an hour before serving. If desired, top each serving with croutons.

Calories: 58　　Total fat: 0 g　　Protein: 2 g
Carbohydrate: 12 g　　Cholesterol: 0 g　　Sodium: 34 mg

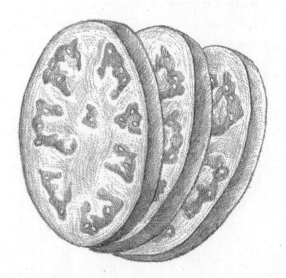

Zesty Green Gazpacho

6 servings

A splendid no-cook soup that will awaken taste buds dulled by summer heat. This soup can be eaten as soon as it is made, but definitely benefits from having time to stand for several hours or overnight so that the lively flavors can mingle. This soup is a great first course for a Mexican or Southwestern-style meal.

2 large cucumbers, peeled, quartered
   lengthwise, and seeded
1 large green bell pepper
6 romaine or green-leaf lettuce leaves,
   coarsely chopped
2 scallions, coarsely chopped
⅓ cup fresh cilantro leaves
1 4-ounce can chopped mild green chilies
   or ½ cup store-bought salsa verde
   (tomatillo sauce)
Juice of 1 lime
1 teaspoon ground cumin
3 cups buttermilk or 1 cup reduced-fat
   sour cream and 2 cups low-fat milk,
   or more as needed
Salt and freshly ground pepper to taste

Reserve about half of one cucumber and half of the bell pepper and set aside. Coarsely chop the rest and place in a food processor along with the lettuce leaves, scallions, and cilantro. Process until pureed with a little texture remaining. Transfer to a large serving container.

Chop and stir in the reserved cucumber and bell pepper, then add the chilies or salsa verde, lime juice, cumin, and buttermilk or sour cream–milk combination. Stir well to combine. Add more buttermilk or low-fat milk if needed to achieve a slightly thick consistency. Season to taste with salt and pepper. Serve at once or cover and chill for several hours or overnight.

Calories: 76	Total fat: 1 g	Protein: 5 g
Carbohydrate: 11 g	Cholesterol: 5 g	Sodium: 66 mg

Sweet-and-Sour Red Cabbage Soup

6 to 8 servings

This refreshing soup is reminiscent of a cold beet borscht. A food processor will make all the grating easier, though the cabbage may be shredded by hand.

1 medium onion, quartered and thinly sliced or grated
2 medium apples, peeled, cored, and grated
1 large carrot, peeled and grated
¾ small head red cabbage, finely shredded
2 cups apple juice
¼ cup apple cider vinegar
¼ cup dry red wine
3 tablespoons brown sugar, or to taste
Salt to taste
Reduced-fat sour cream or plain low-fat yogurt for topping, optional

Combine the first 5 ingredients in a soup pot with enough water to cover and bring to a simmer. As the liquid is heating up, add the vinegar, wine, and brown sugar. Simmer over low heat, covered, until the vegetables are tender, about 40 minutes. Stir in the salt and allow the soup to cool to room temperature. Refrigerate the soup for at least an hour before serving. Top each serving with a scoop of sour cream or yogurt if you'd like.

| Calories: 99 | Total fat: 0 g | Protein: 1 g |
| Carbohydrate: 18 g | Cholesterol: 0 g | Sodium: 13 mg |

An idealist is one who, on noticing that a rose smells better than a cabbage, concludes that it will also make a better soup.

— H. L. Mencken (1880–1956)
Chrestomantry

Spiced Summer Fruit Soup

6 or more servings

This and the following berry soup are the only fruit soups here that need a bit of cooking. The wine and spices give them a wonderfully complex flavor.

1 medium sweet apple, peeled, cored, and finely diced
½ pint (1 cup) fresh blueberries
2 sweet red plums, diced
3 medium ripe peaches, diced
1 cup seedless red or green grapes
1 cup hulled and chopped strawberries
Juice of ½ lemon
4½ cups apple juice
1 2-inch stick cinnamon
5 whole cloves
⅓ cup semisweet red wine
3 to 4 tablespoons light brown sugar, to taste

Combine all the ingredients in a soup pot. Bring to a simmer, then simmer gently, covered, for 20 to 25 minutes, until the fruit is tender. Allow the soup to cool, then refrigerate until chilled. If the soup is too dense, adjust the consistency with more apple juice.

| Calories: 123 | Total fat: 0 g | Protein: 1 g |
| Carbohydrate: 124 g | Cholesterol: 0 g | Sodium: 35 mg |

He that would have the fruit must climb the tree.

— Thomas Fuller
Gnomologia, 1732

Chilled Berry Soup

6 servings

1 pint blueberries
1 pint strawberries, hulled and coarsely
    chopped
1 cup raspberries
2 medium peaches or nectarines, chopped
4 cups raspberry or cranberry juice (made
    from concentrate)
⅓ cup dry red or white wine
Juice of ½ lemon
1 teaspoon cinnamon
½ teaspoon ground allspice
¼ teaspoon ground nutmeg
Brown sugar, honey, or rice syrup to taste,
    if needed
Sliced strawberries for garnish

Combine all the ingredients except the last 2 in a soup pot. Bring to a simmer, then simmer gently, covered, for 10 to 15 minutes, or until the fruit is tender. Remove from the heat.

Taste to see whether a bit more sweetness is needed and add brown sugar, honey, or rice syrup accordingly — depending on the sweetness of the fruit and the fruit juice, you may not wish to add more sweetness at all, or very little. Allow the soup to cool to room temperature, then refrigerate until thoroughly chilled. Garnish each serving with a few strawberry slices.

Calories: 168	Total fat: 0 g	Protein: 1 g
Carbohydrate: 38 g	Cholesterol: 0 g	Sodium: 11 mg

Strawberry-Buttermilk Soup

6 servings

This super-quick no-cook soup is delicious enough to serve as a dessert.

1 quart ripe, sweet strawberries, washed,
    hulled, and cut into approximately
    ½-inch chunks
1 cup apple juice
2 cups buttermilk
¼ cup dry or semisweet red wine
3 to 4 tablespoons honey, or to taste
¼ teaspoon cinnamon
Fresh mint leaves for garnish, optional

Crush a scant cup of the strawberries, then combine them with the cut strawberries and the remaining ingredients, except for the mint leaves, in a serving container. Refrigerate for an hour or so before serving. If desired, garnish each serving with a few mint leaves.

| Calories: 127 | Total fat: 0 g | Protein: 3 g |
| Carbohydrate: 24 g | Cholesterol: 3 g | Sodium: 45 mg |

On strawberries: Doubtless God could have made a better berry, but doubtless God never did.

— William Butler (1835–1902)

Chilled Cantaloupe Soup

6 servings

It takes minutes to make this sweet soup. Try serving it after a meal rather than before — it's a wonderful palate cooler after a spicy meal. Or it can be the main event at lunch on a hot summer day, served with blueberry muffins.

8 heaping cups lush, ripe cantaloupe, cut into 2-inch chunks, divided
1½ cups freshly squeezed orange juice
Juice of ½ to 1 lemon, to taste
2 to 3 tablespoons honey, to taste, depending on the sweetness of the cantaloupe
¼ cup semidry white wine, optional
Pinch each cinnamon and nutmeg
1 cup strawberries, hulled, halved, and sliced
Mint leaves for garnish, optional

Set aside about 2 cups of the melon chunks and place the rest in a food processor or blender. Process until smoothly pureed, then add the orange and lemon juice, honey, optional wine, and spices. Process again until thoroughly blended. Transfer the mixture to a serving container.

Cut the reserved melon chunks into ½-inch dice and stir them into the soup along with the strawberries. Cover and chill for at least an hour before serving. Garnish each serving with 2 or 3 mint leaves if desired.

Calories: 158   Total fat: 0 g   Protein: 3 g
Carbohydrate: 35 g   Cholesterol: 0 g   Sodium: 24 mg

Melon Medley

6 servings

A perfect no-fat dessert soup to make in July, when melons are at their sweetest. This is a refreshing finish to a grilled meal.

3 cups watermelon, cut into ½-inch dice
    and seeded
3 cups honeydew melon, cut into
    ½-inch dice
1 medium cantaloupe, very ripe, seeds
    removed and cut into large chunks
1 pint vanilla or lemon nonfat frozen
    yogurt (or substitute nondairy frozen
    dessert)
2 cups orange juice, preferably fresh
Blueberries for garnish
Mint leaves for garnish

To make part of this soup ahead of time, prepare the watermelon and honeydew as directed, combine in a mixing bowl, then cover and refrigerate. Place the cantaloupe chunks in a separate container; cover and chill.

Just before serving, combine the cantaloupe, frozen yogurt, and orange juice in a food processor and process, in batches if necessary, until smoothly pureed. Divide among 6 serving bowls. Place approximately 1 cup of the watermelon and honeydew mixture in each. Scatter some blueberries over the top of each serving and garnish with 2 or 3 mint leaves.

Calories: 189   Total fat: 2 g   Protein: 4 g
Carbohydrate: 39 g   Cholesterol: 7 g   Sodium: 42 mg

Friends are like melons,
Shall I tell you why?
To find one good
You must a hundred try.

— Claude Mermet, 1600

Minted Peach Soup

6 servings

2½ pounds ripe, juicy peaches, pitted
2 cups orange juice
1 cup buttermilk
1 teaspoon vanilla extract
½ teaspoon ground ginger
Dash of nutmeg
2 tablespoons crushed fresh mint leaves or
    1 mint tea bag
½ cup boiling water
1 to 2 tablespoons honey, or to taste

**A little peach in an orchard
    grew,**
— A little peach of emerald hue,
**Warmed by the sun and wet by
    the dew,**
It grew.

— Eugene Field
   "The Little Peach," 1889

Dice about 2 cups of the peaches and set aside. Place the rest in a food processor or blender along with the juice, buttermilk, vanilla, and spices. Process until smoothly pureed, then transfer to a serving container.

In a cup or small bowl, steep the fresh mint leaves or mint tea in the boiling water for 10 to 15 minutes. Remove the leaves or tea bag and stir the water into the peach soup along with the reserved peaches. Add honey to taste.

Refrigerate for an hour or two to allow the flavors to blend. Before serving, stir the soup and adjust the consistency if necessary with more orange juice.

| Calories: 172 | Total fat: 0 g | Protein: 3 g |
| Carbohydrate: 30 g | Cholesterol: 2 g | Sodium: 19 mg |

Vanilla Fruit Cup Soup

6 servings

Requiring no cooking and no blending, this soup is basically a colorful fruit salad easily transformed into an appealing dessert soup. Use the lush fruits of midsummer for best results.

2 cups berries, as desired (blueberries, raspberries, or chopped strawberries, or a combination)

½ medium cantaloupe, cut into ½ inch dice

2 cups pitted watermelon, cut into ½-inch dice

1½ cups green seedless grapes, left whole if small or halved if large

2 peaches or nectarines, cut into ½-inch dice

2 cups low-fat or nonfat vanilla yogurt

1 teaspoon vanilla extract

¼ teaspoon powdered ginger

1½ cups white grape juice, or as needed

1 to 2 tablespoons honey, optional

Combine all the ingredients except the last two in a serving container. Add enough white grape juice to achieve a slightly thick consistency. Taste, and if you desire extra sweetness, add honey to your liking. Cover and chill for 2 hours or so before serving.

Calories: 216	Total fat: 1 g	Protein: 6 g
Carbohydrate: 43 g	Cholesterol: 5 g	Sodium: 70 mg

Fruit, as it was our primitive and most excellent as well as most innocent food, whilst it grew in Paradise...so it has still preserved, and retained no small tincture of its original and celestial virtue.

— John Evelyn
Complete Gard'ner, 1693

A·C·C·O·M·P·A·N·I-
M·E·N·T·S

Here is a selection of quick breads, muffins, scones, dumplings, and such to accompany your soups. Most are very easy and should ideally be made while the soup is simmering so that they can be served fresh and warm.

Quick Sunflower-Cheese Bread

Makes 1 loaf

This tasty bread goes well with many soups but is especially good with mixed vegetable soups and tomato-based soups.

2 cups whole wheat pastry flour
1½ teaspoons baking powder
1 teaspoon baking soda
½ teaspoon salt
2 egg whites, beaten
1 cup plain low-fat yogurt
2 tablespoons honey
1 teaspoon prepared mustard
1 cup firmly packed grated low-fat cheddar
    cheese or cheddar-style soy cheese
3 tablespoons toasted sunflower seeds

Preheat the oven to 350 degrees.

Combine the first 4 ingredients in a mixing bowl. In another bowl, beat together the egg whites, yogurt, honey, and mustard. Combine the wet ingredients with the dry, stirring vigorously until thoroughly mixed. Stir in the cheese and sunflower seeds.

Pour the batter into a lightly oiled 9-by-5-by-3-inch loaf pan. Bake for 45 minutes, or until the top looks golden brown and crusty. When the loaf pan is cool enough to handle, remove the loaf, place it on a rack, and allow it to cool somewhat before slicing.

Per slice (12 slices per loaf):

Calories: 138	Total fat: 3 g	Protein: 7 g
Carbohydrate: 19 g	Cholesterol: 8 g	Sodium: 193 mg

Green Chili Cornbread

Makes 1 9-inch pan bread

This moist cornbread is an ideal companion to bean soups.

1½ cups cornmeal
½ cup unbleached white flour
¼ cup wheat germ
1 teaspoon baking soda
½ teaspoon baking powder
1 teaspoon salt
2 egg whites, beaten
1 cup reduced-fat sour cream or plain
   low-fat yogurt
2 tablespoons canola oil
1 4-ounce can chopped mild or medium-
   hot green chilies
½ cup thawed frozen corn kernels,
   optional

Preheat the oven to 400 degrees.

Combine the first 6 ingredients in a mixing bowl. In another mixing bowl combine the beaten egg with the sour cream or yogurt and oil. Stir together until smooth.

Make a well in the center of the dry ingredients. Pour in the wet mixture and stir together until combined. Stir in the chilies and optional corn kernels. Pour the mixture into an oiled 9-inch-square baking pan. Bake for 20 to 25 minutes, or until the top is golden and a knife inserted in the center tests clean. Let cool slightly; cut into squares and serve warm.

Per square (12 squares per pan):

Calories: 141	Total fat: 5 g	Protein: 4 g
Carbohydrate: 19 g	Cholesterol: 1 g	Sodium: 195 mg

Pray let me, an American, inform the gentleman, who seems ignorant of the matter, that Indian corn, take it all in all, is one of the most agreeable and wholesome grains in the world.

— Benjamin Franklin (1706–1790)

Savory Bean Bread

Makes 1 9-inch pan bread

A robust bread studded with beans and scallions, this is great with hearty vegetable soups and stews.

1½ cups whole wheat pastry flour
½ cup cornmeal
1 teaspoon baking soda
1 teaspoon baking powder
1 teaspoon salt
½ teaspoon ground cumin
2 egg whites or 1 egg, beaten
1 tablespoon light brown sugar
1 cup plain low-fat yogurt or reduced-fat
    sour cream
¼ cup low-fat milk
1 cup canned pink or pinto beans,
    drained and rinsed
3 scallions, thinly sliced

Preheat the oven to 375 degrees.

Combine the first 6 ingredients in a mixing bowl. In another bowl, combine the beaten egg with the brown sugar, yogurt or sour cream, and milk. Stir together until smooth.

Make a well in the center of the dry ingredients. Pour in the wet mixture and stir together until combined. Gently stir in the beans and scallions. Pour the mixture into an oiled 9-inch-square baking pan. Bake for 20 to 25 minutes, or until the top is golden and a knife inserted in the center tests clean. Let cool slightly; cut into squares and serve warm.

Per square (12 squares per pan):
Calories: 112   Total fat: 0 g   Protein: 5 g
Carbohydrate: 21 g   Cholesterol: 2 g   Sodium: 205 mg

Tomato-Olive Bread

Makes 1 loaf

An unusual bread that teams beautifully with many types of soup. Use your favorite kind of olive; it works well with most any variety.

2¼ cups whole wheat pastry flour
¼ cup wheat germ
2 teaspoons baking powder
½ teaspoon salt
2 egg whites, beaten
1 14-ounce can diced tomatoes, undrained
1 tablespoon light brown sugar
1 tablespoon canola oil
½ cup finely chopped pitted olives, any variety
1 to 2 scallions, minced
½ teaspoon ground cumin
¼ teaspoon dried basil
Pinch of dried thyme

Preheat the oven to 350 degrees.

Combine the first 4 ingredients in a bowl and stir together. In another bowl, combine the beaten egg with the tomatoes, brown sugar, and oil. Pour the wet ingredients into the dry and stir together just until well mixed.

Stir in the remaining ingredients, then pour the batter into a lightly oiled 9-by-5-by-3-inch loaf pan. Bake for 45 to 50 minutes, or until a knife inserted into the center of the loaf tests clean. Let cool until just warm, then cut into slices to serve.

Per slice (12 slices per loaf):

Calories: 116	Total fat: 3 g	Protein: 4 g
Carbohydrate: 18 g	Cholesterol: 0 g	Sodium: 144 mg

Except the vine, there is no plant which bears a fruit of as great an importance as the olive.

— Pliny
Historia Naturalis, 79 B.C.

Focaccia Bread

Makes 1 round loaf

Although this excellent traditional Italian bread is yeasted, it does not take as long to make as other yeasted breads since it only requires one rather brief rising. If you are making a long-simmering soup, this bread will likely fit into the time frame.

1 package active dry yeast
1 cup warm water
1 tablespoon light brown sugar
¼ cup olive oil, divided
1½ cups whole wheat flour
1 cup unbleached white flour
1 teaspoon salt
1 tablespoon minced fresh garlic
Coarse salt
Dried oregano or rosemary

Pour the yeast into the warm water and let stand to dissolve for 5 to 10 minutes. Stir in the brown sugar and half of the olive oil. In a large mixing bowl, combine the flours and salt. Work the yeast mixture in using your hands, then turn out onto a well-floured board. Knead for 5 minutes, adding more flour if the dough is too sticky. Shape into a round and roll out into a circle with a 12-inch diameter.

Place on an oiled and floured baking sheet, cover with a tea towel, and let rise in a warm place for 30 to 40 minutes. When the dough has finished rising, poke shallow holes into its surface with your fingers at even intervals. Sprinkle the remaining olive oil over the top evenly, followed by the garlic, coarse salt, and herbs.

Bake in a preheated 400-degree oven for 20 to 25 minutes, or until the bread is golden on top and sounds hollow when tapped. Serve warm, cut into wedges, or just have everyone break off pieces.

Per wedge (8 wedges per loaf):

Calories: 192	Total fat: 7 g	Protein: 5 g
Carbohydrate: 27 g	Cholesterol: 0 g	Sodium: 269 mg

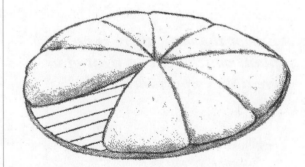

Whole Wheat Vegetable Muffins

Makes 1 dozen

Tiny bits of fresh vegetables give these muffins a special flavor and texture. They are particularly good with pureed soups and cheese soups.

1 cup assorted fresh vegetables, cut into 1-inch chunks (choose from among carrot, green pepper, radish, cabbage, and zucchini)
2 egg whites, beaten
2 tablespoons canola oil
2 tablespoons honey
¾ cup plain low-fat yogurt
¼ cup low-fat milk
1 teaspoon finely grated onion
1½ cups whole wheat flour
½ cup unbleached white flour
1½ teaspoons baking powder
½ teaspoon salt
Poppy seeds for topping, optional

Preheat the oven to 350 degrees.

Place the vegetable chunks in a food processor. Pulse on and off until the vegetables are finely minced; take care not to overprocess. Set aside.

In a mixing bowl, combine the beaten egg whites with the oil, honey, yogurt, milk, and onion. Stir together and add the minced vegetables.

In another bowl, combine the flours, baking powder, and salt. Add the wet ingredients to the dry and stir together until well blended. Divide the mixture among 12 lightly oiled or paper-lined muffin tins. Top with the optional poppy seeds. Bake for 20 to 25 minutes, or until the tops are golden brown. Remove the muffins from the tins as soon as they are cool enough to handle and cool them on a rack or a plate.

Calories: 112   Total fat: 2 g   Protein: 4 g
Carbohydrate: 18 g   Cholesterol: 1 g   Sodium: 112 mg

Cheese and Herb Corn Muffins

Makes 1 dozen

Moist and flavorful, these muffins are especially nice with bean soups.

⅔ cup cornmeal
1 cup whole wheat pastry flour
1 teaspoon baking powder
½ teaspoon baking soda
½ teaspoon salt
2 egg whites or 1 egg, beaten
3 tablespoons canola oil
1 cup buttermilk
1 cup grated reduced-fat cheddar cheese
½ cup cooked fresh or thawed frozen
   corn kernels
3 tablespoons mixed fresh herbs, minced,
   or 1½ teaspoons mixed dried herbs
   of your choice

Preheat the oven to 400 degrees.

Combine the first 5 ingredients in a mixing bowl. In another bowl, combine the beaten egg with the oil and buttermilk. Combine the wet and dry ingredients and stir until thoroughly mixed. Stir in the grated cheese and herbs.

Divide the batter among 12 lightly oiled or paper-lined muffin tins. Bake for 12 to 15 minutes, or until the muffins are golden brown and a toothpick inserted into the center of one tests clean. Cool on a rack, then store in an airtight container as soon as the muffins are at room temperature.

| Calories: 132 | Total fat: 5 g | Protein: 6 g |
| Carbohydrate: 14 g | Cholesterol: 8 g | Sodium: 176 mg |

Her hair that lay along her back
Was yellow like ripe corn.

— Dante Gabriel Rossetti (1828–82)
The Blessed Damozel

Buttermilk Oat Muffins

Makes 1 dozen

Tender and just slightly sweet, these are good teamed with spicy or chunky soups and stews.

1¼ cups whole wheat flour
¾ cup rolled oats
1½ teaspoons baking powder
½ teaspoon baking soda
½ teaspoon salt
2 egg whites, beaten
1 cup buttermilk
3 tablespoons honey
2 tablespoons canola oil

Preheat the oven to 350 degrees.

Combine the first 5 ingredients in a mixing bowl and stir together. In another bowl, beat together the remaining ingredients. Slowly pour the wet ingredients into the dry and stir vigorously until well combined.

Divide the batter among 12 lightly oiled or paper-lined muffin tins. Bake for 15 to 20 minutes, or until the tops of the muffins are golden and a toothpick inserted into the center of one tests clean. Cool on a rack, then store in an airtight container as soon as the muffins are at room temperature.

| Calories: 110 | Total fat: 3 g | Protein: 4 g |
| Carbohydrate: 17 g | Cholesterol: 1 g | Sodium: 109 mg |

*Five muffins are enough
for any man at a meal.*

— E. V. Knox (1881–1971)
Gorgeous Times

Barley or Rice Triangles

Makes about 20 to 22

These offbeat little griddle breads pair well with bean soups, cheese soups, and pureed soups.

1¼ cups whole wheat pastry flour
¼ cup cornmeal
1 teaspoon baking powder
1 teaspoon salt
3 tablespoons soy margarine, softened
1 cup well-cooked barley or brown rice
¼ cup low-fat milk or soy milk, or as
    needed

Combine the first 4 ingredients in a mixing bowl and stir together. Cut the margarine into bits and blend into the flour mixture with the tines of a fork or a pastry blender until the mixture resembles coarse crumbs. Stir in the cooked barley or rice, then add enough milk or soy milk so that the mixture holds together as a firm dough, working it together with your hands.

Divide the dough into 2 parts. On a well-floured board, roll out one part until it is ¼ inch thick. With a sharp knife, cut the dough into triangular pieces with approximately 2-inch sides. Repeat with the remaining dough; gather up any dough left over from cutting and roll out again until it is all used up.

Heat a griddle or large nonstick skillet that has been coated with cooking oil spray. Bake the triangles over moderate heat until they are touched with light brown on both sides. Transfer to a plate to cool, and once the triangles are at room temperature, store them in a covered container.

Calories: 53	Total fat: 2 g	Protein: 1 g
Carbohydrate: 8 g	Cholesterol: 0 g	Sodium: 123 mg

Cheddar-Oat Griddle Biscuits

Makes about 20

The tang of cheddar cheese contrasts well with mildly flavored soups such as "Cream" of Cauliflower Soup (page 83).

1 cup whole wheat pastry flour
1 cup rolled oats
1 teaspoon salt
1 teaspoon baking powder
3 tablespoons soy margarine, softened
1 cup grated reduced-fat cheddar cheese
¼ cup low-fat milk, or as needed

The oat is the Horatio Alger of cereals, which has progressed, if not from rags to riches, at least from weed to health food.

— Waverly Root
Food, 1980

Combine the first 4 ingredients in a mixing bowl. Cut the margarine into bits, then work into the flour-oat mixture with the tines of a fork or a pastry blender until the mixture resembles coarse crumbs. Stir in the cheddar cheese, then add enough milk to form a stiff dough, using your hands to work it together. Turn out onto a well-floured board and roll the dough out to a ¼-inch thickness. Cut the dough into 2-inch rounds using a cookie cutter or a glass. Gather up leftover dough and roll out again until all the dough is used up.

Heat a griddle or a large nonstick skillet that has been sprayed with cooking oil spray. Bake the biscuits on both sides over medium heat until golden brown. Cool on a plate, then transfer to a covered container when cooled to room temperature.

Calories: 71	Total fat: 3 g	Protein: 3 g
Carbohydrate: 7 g	Cholesterol: 4 g	Sodium: 169 mg

Potato-Rye Griddle Biscuits

Makes 16 to 18

These are especially good with soups containing beets, cabbage, or strong greens.

1 cup rye flour
¾ cup unbleached white flour
1 teaspoon baking powder
1 teaspoon salt
1 teaspoon caraway seeds, optional
1 cup well-mashed cooked potato, chilled
2 egg whites, beaten
3 tablespoons canola oil

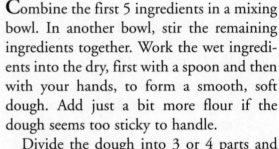

Combine the first 5 ingredients in a mixing bowl. In another bowl, stir the remaining ingredients together. Work the wet ingredients into the dry, first with a spoon and then with your hands, to form a smooth, soft dough. Add just a bit more flour if the dough seems too sticky to handle.

Divide the dough into 3 or 4 parts and roll each out to ¼-inch thickness on a floured board. Cut with the rim of a 2-inch round glass or cookie cutter. Knead together the leftover parts of the dough and roll out again until it is all used up.

Heat a large nonstick skillet or griddle that has been coated with cooking oil spray. Bake each round over medium heat for 5 to 7 minutes on each side, or until golden. Serve warm.

Calories: 71	Total fat: 2 g	Protein: 2 g
Carbohydrate: 10 g	Cholesterol: 0 g	Sodium: 132 mg

Onion-Rye Oven Scones

Makes 8

Moist and slightly crumbly, these scones team especially well with soups made of root vegetables — potatoes, parsnips, and the like.

1½ cups rye flour
¾ cup unbleached white flour
2 teaspoons baking powder
1 teaspoon salt
3 tablespoons soy margarine, softened
4 egg whites, beaten
2 tablespoons molasses, honey, or brown rice syrup
¼ cup low-fat milk or soy milk, or as needed

Topping:
2 teaspoons canola oil
1 medium onion, quartered and thinly sliced
Poppy seeds

Preheat the oven to 350 degrees.

Combine the first 4 ingredients in a mixing bowl. Cut the margarine into the flour mixture with a pastry blender or the tines of a fork until the mixture resembles a coarse meal.

In another bowl, combine the eggs and molasses, honey, or rice syrup. Work into the flour mixture, followed by enough milk or soy milk to form a soft dough. Transfer the dough to a well-floured board and knead briefly with floured hands. Roll into a round 9 inches in diameter and place on a lightly oiled baking sheet. Score the round with a knife, about halfway through the dough, into 8 equal wedge-shaped parts.

For the topping, heat the oil in a small skillet. Add the onion and sauté over moderate heat until lightly browned. Distribute the onion evenly over the scones, then sprinkle with poppy seeds. Bake for 12 to 15 minutes, or until the top is golden. Let cool somewhat before slicing.

Calories: 199	Total fat: 7 g	Protein: 6 g
Carbohydrate: 29 g	Cholesterol: 0 g	Sodium: 353 mg

Sow timely thy white wheat,
  sow rye in the dust,
Let seed have his longing,
  let soil have her lust.
Let rye be partaken of
Michelmas spring,
To bear out the hardness
  that winter doth bring.

— Thomas Tusser
Five Hundred Points of Good Husbandry, 1580

Currant Griddle Scones

8 servings

If you'd like an accompaniment to fruit soups, these slightly sweet scones are just the thing.

1½ cups whole wheat pastry flour
1½ teaspoons baking powder
¼ teaspoon cinnamon
¼ cup soy margarine, softened
¼ cup light brown sugar
¼ cup low-fat milk or soy milk, or as
    needed
⅔ cup dried currants
3 tablespoons finely chopped walnuts

I stamp this kiss
Upon thy currant lips.

— William Shakespeare (1564–1616)

In a mixing bowl, combine the flour with the baking powder and cinnamon. Cut the margarine into bits, then work into the flour with a pastry blender or the tines of a fork until the mixture resembles coarse crumbs. Stir in the brown sugar, then add enough milk or soy milk to hold the dough together. It should be a light, nonsticky dough. Work the currants and walnuts in with your hands, then turn the dough out onto a well-floured board and knead briefly.

Form the dough into a ball, then roll out into a round about 10 inches in diameter and ½ inch thick. Cut into 8 even wedge shapes, then arrange on a heated griddle that has been coated with cooking oil spray. Bake on both sides over medium heat, about 8 to 10 minutes per side, or until golden brown. Cool on a rack and serve warm.

Calories: 197	Total fat: 8 g	Protein: 4 g
Carbohydrate: 28 g	Cholesterol: 0 g	Sodium: 75 mg

Scallion Logs

Makes about 20

These tasty little breads are ideal with Oriental-style soups.

1½ cups whole wheat pastry flour
1 tablespoon sesame seeds
½ teaspoon baking powder
2 egg whites, beaten
2 tablespoons canola oil
1 tablespoon soy sauce or tamari
2 to 3 scallions, green parts only, minced

Combine the flour, sesame seeds, and baking powder in a mixing bowl. In a small mixing bowl, combine the beaten egg whites with the oil, soy sauce or tamari, and scallions.

Work the wet and dry mixtures together, using the hands once fairly well combined, to form a stiff dough. With floured hands, tear off small bits of dough and roll between the palms to make finger-shaped logs about 3 inches long.

Coat the bottom of a large nonstick skillet with cooking oil spray and heat over medium-high heat. Gently arrange the logs in the skillet and cook them, turning on all sides until golden brown, about 5 to 7 minutes. When done, arrange on a plate. Serve at once, if possible, and store any that are left over in a tightly covered container.

Calories: 47	Total fat: 2 g	Protein: 2 g
Carbohydrate: 6	Cholesterol: 0 g	Sodium: 56 mg

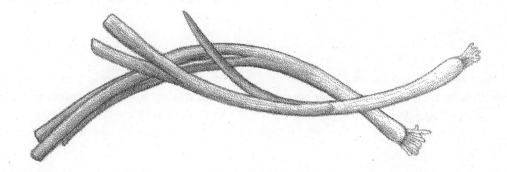

Chapatis

Makes 12

These simple, traditional Indian flatbreads are appropriate served with curried soups and stews.

1 cup whole wheat flour
1 cup unbleached white flour
¾ cups water, or as needed
½ teaspoon salt

Combine the flours and salt in a mixing bowl and stir together. Add water a bit at a time until the dough holds together. Turn out onto a floured board and knead for about 5 minutes, or until smooth and elastic. Place the dough in a small floured bowl and cover with a clean tea towel. Let the dough rest for 30 minutes.

Divide the dough into 12 even-sized balls. Heat a small nonstick skillet. Roll out each ball of dough into a thin round. Cook on the skillet over medium heat until touched with light brown spots, about 3 to 4 minutes. Flip and cook on the other side; repeat with the other balls of dough. Keep the chapatis warm, stacked one atop another in foil, until all are done. Serve at once.

Calories: 67	Total fat: 0 g	Protein: 2 g
Carbohydrate: 14 g	Cholesterol: 0 g	Sodium: 179 mg

Parmesan Pita Wedges

Here's a really quick-to-fix idea, yielding good results with little effort. These are especially appropriate with Italian-style soups.

Pita bread (store bought), preferably
    whole wheat, allowing 1 pita per serving
Extra-virgin olive oil
Grated fresh Parmesan cheese
Dried oregano, optional

Preheat the oven to 350 degrees.

Cut each pita into 4 wedges. Arrange on 1 or 2 baking sheets and brush the tops with olive oil. Sprinkle with Parmesan cheese and optional oregano. Bake for 5 minutes. Serve at once.

Calories: 140	Total fat: 1 g	Protein: 2 g
Carbohydrate: 30 g	Cholesterol: 1 g	Sodium: 16 mg

Garlic Croutons

This idea is so simple that it scarcely qualifies as a recipe, yet there are few embellishments for soup that are as simple and that seem to please everyone so much. It's also a good way to use up bread that may otherwise go stale.

Ends and pieces of whole grain bread, several days old, allowing about 1 small slice per serving
1 clove garlic, cut in half lengthwise

Rub each piece of bread on both sides with the open side of the garlic clove. Cut the bread into approximately ½-inch dice. Discard the garlic or use for another purpose.

Prepare the croutons in one of the two following ways: Arrange on a baking sheet and bake in a 275-degree oven for 20 minutes or so, until dry and crisp. Or, if the weather is warm and you don't wish to use the oven, simply toast the croutons in a heavy skillet over moderate heat, stirring frequently, about 20 minutes, or until dry and crisp.

Allow the croutons to cool on a plate. They may be used as soon as they have cooled, but if you can leave them out at room temperature for at least 30 minutes or so, they'll stay crisper in soup.

Calories: 89   Total fat: 0 g   Protein: 3 g
Carbohydrate: 18 g   Cholesterol: 0 g   Sodium: 177 mg

It is not an exaggeration to say that peace and happiness begin, geographically, where garlic is used in cooking.

— X. Marcel Boulestin (1878–1943)

Bruschetta

This Italian recipe for wide garlicky toasts is a great all-purpose accompaniment for almost any type of soup (except for fruit soups). In the traditional recipe, olive oil is drizzled or brushed on the toasts, but I leave this as an option.

1 large rounded (rather than long and
    narrow) fresh Italian bread
1 large clove garlic, halved
Olive oil, optional

Bread made from pure wheat flour ... finely moulded and baked, comforteth and strengtheneth the heart, and maketh a man fat, and preserveth health.

— William Vaughn
Directions for Health, 1600

Preheat the oven to 350 degrees.

Cut the bread into approximately ¾-inch thick slices. Place them on a nonstick baking sheet and bake for 10 to 15 minutes, turning once, or until both sides are golden and crisp. Or, you may place them right on the oven rack, in which case they need not be turned. Watch them carefully!

Remove the toasts from the oven. When cool enough to handle, rub one side of each toast with the open side of the garlic. If desired, brush a bit of olive oil on one side of the toasts as well.

| Calories: 89 | Total fat: 0 g | Protein: 3 g |
| Carbohydrate: 18 g | Cholesterol: 0 g | Sodium: 177 mg |

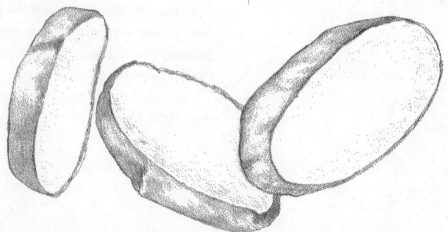

Cornmeal Dumplings

Makes about 20 to 22

If you've never made dumplings, you'll be surprised at how easy they are to make. They add substance and textural interest to many types of soup. These cornmeal dumplings go well in bean soups and tomato-based soups.

⅔ cup cornmeal
⅔ cup whole wheat pastry flour
1 teaspoon baking powder
1 teaspoon salt
Several grindings of fresh pepper
2 eggs or 4 egg whites
2 tablespoons canola oil
4 to 5 tablespoons low-fat milk or
    soy milk
10 cups water

Combine the first 4 ingredients in a mixing bowl, then add a few grindings of pepper. In another bowl, beat the eggs together with the oil. Work the egg-oil mixture into the flour mixture, then add just enough milk or soy milk to make the mixture adhesive but not too loose. Shape into balls approximately ¾ inch in diameter.

Bring the water to a rolling boil in a soup pot. Carefully drop each dumpling in and cook at a steady simmer for 15 minutes, then remove with a slotted spoon. Drain and serve in soup at once, or cool and refrigerate, then warm up in a soup when needed.

Per dumpling:

Calories: 52	Total fat: 2 g	Protein: 1 g
Carbohydrate: 6 g	Cholesterol: 20 g	Sodium: 108 mg

Oat-Chive Dumplings

Makes 14 to 16

These add a nice touch to bean soups, vegetable soups, and pureed soups.

⅔ cup fine oatmeal
⅔ cup unbleached white flour
2 tablespoons wheat germ
1 teaspoon salt
2 egg whites
1 tablespoon canola oil
2 tablespoons finely snipped chives
Several grindings of pepper
2 to 3 tablespoons low-fat milk or
  soy milk
10 cups water

Combine the oatmeal, flour, wheat germ, and salt in a mixing bowl. In another bowl, beat the egg whites together with the oil, chives, and pepper, then work into the oatmeal mixture. Add enough milk or soy milk to form a stiff dough. Shape into balls about ¾ inch in diameter.

Bring the water to a rolling boil in a large saucepan. Carefully drop each dumpling in and cook at a steady simmer for 15 minutes. Drain and serve in soup at once, or cool and refrigerate, then warm up in a soup when needed.

Per dumpling:

Calories: 47	Total fat: 1 g	Protein: 2 g
Carbohydrate: 7 g	Cholesterol: 0 g	Sodium: 150 mg

Oats: A grain which in England is generally given to horses, but which in Scotland supports the people.

— Samuel Johnson
  *Dictionary of the English Language,*1755

Parsley-Potato Dumplings

Makes 14 to 16

Try these tasty dumplings in root vegetable soups, curried soups, and brothy vegetable soups.

⅔ cup whole wheat flour
⅔ cup unbleached white flour
1 teaspoon salt
1 cup cooked, well-mashed potatoes, chilled
2 egg whites, beaten
3 tablespoons minced fresh parsley
10 cups water

Combine the flours and salt in a mixing bowl. In another bowl, combine the mashed potatoes, beaten egg whites, and parsley. Work the wet and dry ingredients together and shape into balls about 1 inch in diameter.

Bring the water to a rolling boil in a large saucepan. Carefully drop the dumplings in. If they seem to stick to the bottom, gently nudge them up with a wooden spoon. Cook at a steady simmer for 15 minutes. Drain and serve in soup at once, or cool and refrigerate, then warm up in a soup when needed.

Per dumpling:

Calories: 49	Total fat: 0 g	Protein: 2 g
Carbohydrate: 10 g	Cholesterol: 0 g	Sodium: 150 mg

Never cut parsley if you are in love. If you give it away, you also give away your luck.

— Old European folk belief

INDEX